The Meeting
by Andrew Payne

SERVING THEATRE

S F

SINCE 1830

WWW.SAMUELFRENCH.CO.UK
WWW.SAMUELFRENCH.COM

Cast

Stratton
Mark Hadfield

Trained at RADA. **Recent theatre includes** *Mrs Henderson Presents* (Theatre Royal Bath); *Matchbox Theatre* (Hampstead Theatre); *Made In Dagenham* (Adelphi Theatre); *Jeeves & Wooster in Perfect Nonsense* (Duke of York's Theatre); *Singin' In The Rain* (Palace Theatre); *Uncle Vanya* (Vaudeville Theatre); *The Tempest* and *Jeffrey Bernard Is Unwell* (Theatre Royal Bath); *The Painkiller* (Lyric Theatre Belfast); *Into The Woods* (Regent's Park); *Talent* and *Rookery Nook* (Menier Chocolate Factory); *The Hour We Knew Nothing of Each Other* and *Therese Raquin* - Olivier Award nomination for Best Supporting Performance (National Theatre). RSC credits include: *Hamlet; Love's Labour's Lost; A Midsummer Night's Dream; The Canterbury Tales; Twelfth Night; Two Gentlemen of Verona; The Seagull* and *Talk of the City*. **Television work includes** *Maigret* (ITV); *From The Cradle To The Grave* (BBC); *Trollied* (Sky); *Wallander* (Left Bank); *Foyle's War* (ITV) and *People Like Us* (BBC). **Film work includes** *A Royal Night Out; Hamlet; A Cock & Bull Story; In The Bleak Midwinter; Mary Shelley's Frankenstein* and *Felicia's Journey*.

Ellen
Rebecca Night

Trained at Rose Bruford and National Youth Theatre. **Theatre work includes** *A Flea in her Ear* (Old Vic); *The Grapes of Wrath* (Chichester Theatre); *Spoonface Steinberg* (Etcetera Theatre); *The Tempest* (Brownsea Open Air) and *The Importance of Being Earnest* (Theatre Royal Bath/ West End). **Television work includes** *Starlings* (Sky); *This September* (Telemunchen); *The Courageous Heart of Irena Sendler* (CBS); *Fanny Hill* (BBC); *Caught In A Trap* (ITV); *Wuthering Heights* (ITV); *Lark Rise to Candleford* (BBC) and *Maigret Sets a Trap* (ITV). **Film work includes** *Suspension of Disbelief; Dartmoor Killing; Leopard; Rebecca; Framed* and *Tail.*

Frank
Malcolm Sinclair

Theatre work includes *The Bloody Irish!* (Helix Theatre, DCU); *Temple* (Donmar); *Pressure* (Chichester/Royal Lyceum); *Quartermaine's Terms* (Wyndham's Theatre); *The Doctor's Dilemma* and *The King James Bible Readings* (National Theatre); *66 Books* (Bush Theatre); *Rattigan's Nijinksy* (Chichester Festival Theatre); *The Habit of Art* and *The Power of Yes* (National Theatre); *Ivanov* (Donmar); *Rosmersholm* (Almeida); *The History Boys* (National Theatre/Broadway); *Richard III* (Royal Shakespeare Company); *Luther; House/ Garden; Richard III; Racing Demon* and *The Misanthrope* (all National Theatre). **Television work includes** *Midsomer Murders* (ITV); *Virtuoso* (HBO); *Tubby and Enid* (Sky); *Worricker* (BBC); *Silk* (BBC); *Henry V* (BBC); *Parade's End* (HBO/BBC); *Material Girl* (Carnival); *Daphne* (BBC) and *Foyle's War* (ITV). **Film work includes** *The Man Who Knew Infinity; A Belfast Story; The Young Victoria; Casino Royale; V for Vendetta; The Statement; Secret Passage; Keep The Aspidistra Flying; Young Poisoner's Handbook* and *God On The Rocks.*

Cole
Sam Swainsbury

Theatre work includes *A Midsummer Night's Dream* and *Privates On Parade* (Michael Grandage Season); *The Taming of the Shrew* (Royal Shakespeare Company); *When Did You Last See My Mother?* (Trafalgar Studios); *The Comedy of Errors* and *Richard III* (Propeller); *Hay Fever* (Rose Theatre, Kingston); *A Day At The Racists* (Finborough Theatre); *The Rivals* (Southwark Playhouse); *The Merchant of Venice/A Midsummer Night's Dream* (Propeller); *Burial At Thebes* (Nottingham Playhouse/Barbican); *Hysteria* (Birmingham Rep) and *Slope* (The Tramway, Glasgow). **Television work includes** *Mum* (BBC); *Atlantis* (BBC); *Call The Midwife* (BBC); *Doctors* (BBC); *Harley Street* (ITV) and *Jekyll* (BBC). **Film work includes** *Amerikan Kanibal; Silent Hill Requiem* and *Thor: The Dark World.*

Creative Team

Writer
Andrew Payne

Andrew Payne's plays include *En Reunion* (Theatre de Montparnasse); *Le Plan B* (Comedie des Champs Elysees); *Shut Up* and *Mugged* (National Theatre Connections); *Squash* and *Then What* (Old Red Lion). Television work includes *Midsomer Murders* (ITV); *DCI Banks* (ITV); *Pie In The Sky* (BBC); *Malice Aforethought* (ITV); *You Me And It* (BBC) and *Minder* (ITV).

Director
Denis Lawson

Apart from his extensive career as an actor in theatre, television and film, Denis is also an experienced theatre director. Denis' directing debut was at Hampstead Theatre in the previous building, *Little Malcolm And His Struggle Against The Eunuchs,* starring his nephew, Ewan McGregor, which transferred to the Pinter Theatre. He subsequently directed *Burning Issues* at Hampstead. His last production was *The Anniversary,* with Sheila Hancock at the Liverpool Playhouse which transferred to the Garrick Theatre. Denis has directed three short films, *The Bass Player, Solid Geometry* and *In The Mix.* He has been running film workshops for working actors for the last twenty years and had a book published last year based on those workshops, *The Actor and The Camera.* He is delighted to be back at Hampstead directing this new play by Andrew Payne, *The Meeting.*

Designer
Alex Marker

Trained at Wimbledon School of Art, Alex is resident designer at the award winning Finborough Theatre, where he has designed nearly forty productions and recently directed a revival of J.B Priestley's *Summer Day's Dream.* Other theatre designs include *Can't Buy Me Love* and *London Calling* (Salisbury Playhouse); *The Man Called*

Monkhouse (Edinburgh/tour); *Asking Rembrandt* (Old Red Lion); *The Trial of Jane Fonda* (Assembly Rooms); *The Cutting of the Cloth* and *What the Women Did* (Southwark Playhouse); *Around the World in 80 Days* (Chipping Norton/tour); *Rift* (Brewhouse); *Ex* (Soho Theatre); *Jus' Like That - An Evening with Tommy Cooper* (national tour) and *The Schools' Theatre Festival* (Young Vic). West End designs include *London Wall* (St James); *Plague Over England* (Duchess); *My Real War 1914- ?*; *Dream of the Dog* and *Tape* (Trafalgar Studios) and a charity gala performance of *Sweet Charity* (Theatre Royal Drury Lane).

Lighting
Neill Brinkworth

Recent theatre work includes *In the Night Garden Live* (Minor/BBC); *The Divided Laing* (Arcola Theatre); *As Is* (Trafalgar Studios); *Sweat Factory* (YMT, Sadlers Wells); *Dido & Aeneas* (English Touring Opera); *The White Feather* (Union Theatre); *Contact.Com* (Park Theatre); *The Cutting of the Cloth; In Lambeth* and *Who do we Think We Are?* (all Southwark Playhouse); *Dessa Rose* (Trafalgar Studios); *Café Chaos* (The Kosh); *The Seagull* (Arcola); *An Enemy of the People* (Albany); *Jephthe* (English Touring Opera); *Strauss Gala* (Raymond Gubbay); *Bridgetower* (City of London Festival/ETO); *Vincent River* (Old Vic productions); *Step 9 of 12* and *Tape* (both Trafalgar Studios); *The Tin Solider* (peut etre); *Prometheus; The Frogs* and *Agamemnon* (all Cambridge Arts Theatre); *Dick Whittington* (Hertford Theatre); *Lean* (Tristan Bates); *Accolade; Don Juan Comes Back from the War* and *Fanta Orange* (all Finborough Theatre); *Seven Pomegranate Seeds* (Oxford Playhouse) and *Six Men & A Poker Game* (Gridiron).

Sound
John Leonard

John has provided soundtracks for theatres worldwide for over forty years. Previous work at Hampstead Theatre includes *Firebird; Mr Foote's Other Leg* (also West End); *Luna Gale, Matchbox Theatre; Stevie; Seminar; Rapture, Blister, Burn;*

Old Money; Farewell to the Theatre; The Mystae; Ecstasy (also West End) and *The Train Driver.* Recent sound designs include *Into The Woods* (Manchester Royal Exchange); *Little Eyolf* (Almeida); *Waste* (National Theatre); *Sweet Charity* (RADA); *McQueen* (West End); *Pig Farm* (St. James'); *Just Jim Dale* (West End); *Ghosts* (Almeida/West End/New York) and *The Duck House* (West End).

The Meeting production team would like to thank Neil Willing at Olleco.

Hampstead Downstairs is supported by The Peter Wolff Trust, Jocelyn Abbey/Joan Abbey Estate, The Eric Abraham Charitable Trust, The Andor Charitable Trust, Celia Atkin, The John S Cohen Foundation, The Garrick Charitable Trust, The Leche Trust, Mr & Mrs V Meyer, MishMosh Media, Simon & Midge Palley and The Sackler Trust.

We would like to thank MishMosh Media for the sponsorship of £5 tickets on 2 February, and for year round support of Hampstead Downstairs

The Meeting

by Andrew Payne

The Meeting was first performed at
Hampstead Downstairs on 27th January 2016.

The cast was as follows:

Stratton	Mark Hadfield
Ellen	Rebecca Night
Frank	Malcolm Sinclair
Cole	Sam Swainsbury

Writer	Andrew Payne
Director	Denis Lawson
Designer	Alex Marker
Lighting	Neill Brinkworth
Sound	John Leonard

For Dudley

CHARACTERS

FRANK – A man in his fifties.
STRATTON – A man in his forties.
COLE – A man in his twenties.
ELLEN – A woman in her thirties.

ONE – Stratton's office, Monday morning.
TWO – Stratton's office, Tuesday morning.
THREE – Stratton's office, Wednesday morning.
FOUR – Rear of Treats, a bar, Wednesday evening.

ONE

An office. A door upstage centre, flanked by bookshelves and cupboards.

Left, a big desk, computer, phones, a high-backed chair. Right, two sofas around a low table.

Enter **STRATTON**, *fortyish, suit, tie, carrying a laptop bag and talking on his mobile. Goes to the desk, puts down his bag. Sniffs the air.*

STRATTON *(into phone)* So then she –

(…)

Wait, wait, was this before or –

STRATTON *goes to a cupboard, takes out a can of air freshener, sprays it around.*

(into phone) She <u>what</u>?

STRATTON *freezes.*

(into phone) In the eye? Christ –

(…)

Darling, what do you mean, 'she didn't exactly hit him'?

(…)

So is he okay?

(…)

Well, of course I'm worried about her, but what –

(…)

1

No, I don't always side with the other –

(…)

Well, you remember what happened with that other boy, whatsisname –

(…)

No, darling, sorry, the teacher said –

(…)

Okay, okay. Okay. I know, I'm sure this is different but –

(…)

Okay, but the thing is, I've got this meeting, this rather important –

(…)

Yes, of course I'll ring the school but I can't now, I've got this, this very, actually rather crucial –

(…)

Okay, okay, I'll –

(…)

I'll –

(…)

I promise –

(…)

Talk later. Bye. Love you. Bye, bye.

(…)

Bye.

STRATTON *hangs up. He returns the air freshener to the cupboard.*

STRATTON *goes to his desk, patting his pockets, looking for something. Checks the desktop, then starts opening drawers, hunting. No luck.* **STRATTON** *picks up his desk phone, punches a single number.*

Lucy, have you seen my pen? You know, the one that my wife –

(…)

Yes, exactly –

(…)

Okay –

(…)

No, no, no, it's probably at home. Thanks, Lucy.

STRATTON *hangs up, starts searching his pockets again. The desk phone rings.* **STRATTON** *grabs it eagerly.*

Have you found it? *(disappointed)*

Oh, okay.

(…)

Yes, put her on…

(…)

Claire, if you're after Jack, he's not here yet, we're seeing him in –

(checks watch)

– in twenty minutes, so –

(…)

What? He what?

(…)

He can't?

The door opens and **COLE** *sticks his head in. Late twenties, casually dressed, earphones, shoulder bag.* **STRATTON** *beckons him in.*

(into phone) – well, it's very short notice –

STRATTON *paces.* **COLE** *sits on one of the sofas, puts his feet up on the table. Takes a laptop out of his bag, opens it.*

– and Cole's already here and we really need to move on with this –

(…)

Yes – no! No, no, totally not your fault. We'll just have to reschedule for tomorrow, then. Why don't you talk to Lucy and – what?

(…)

He's not coming in at all?

STRATTON *has moved over behind* **COLE** *on the sofa. He pulls out one of* **COLE**'s *earphones to get his attention.*

Jack isn't coming in at all?

(…)

Jack's <u>gone</u>?

(…)

You mean 'gone' as in –

(…)

– as in 'gone', right.

(…)

They what?

(…)

My God.

(…)

So, so, what do we, where does that leave us? Because we were about to –

(…)

Okay, but we've been working on this, me and Jack – *(a look from* **COLE***)*

– and Cole – we've been working on this for – for –

(…)

– exactly, and Jack has just been fantastic, so, you know, I'm a little concerned by the whole, I mean, where is he? Can I call him, give him my – what?

(…)

Really? My God. Well, okay, if that's the, the –

(…)

Okay, right, right. Okay, thanks.

STRATTON *hangs up.*

COLE What?

STRATTON Jack's not coming in.

COLE What, he's ill or something?

STRATTON No, he's gone.

COLE Gone? How do you mean, gone?

STRATTON Gone! This morning, first thing. He was escorted, security escorted him off the, off the –

COLE Jack? Security escorted Jack?

STRATTON – they marched him out, they had him by the arms apparently –

COLE What did he do, Stratt?

STRATTON I don't know, he can't talk, there's an injunction, he can't talk to anyone, there's a, a, I don't know, a confidentiality thing, we can't call him or, or –

COLE What the fuck did he do?

STRATTON I don't know! We have to make some calls, find out what the, the –

COLE – so the meeting's off –

STRATTON I'll have to, I'll have to talk to Frank, see what he, see what we –

COLE So the meeting's off –

STRATTON They're going to call me back and reschedule –

COLE How can they reschedule if Jack's gone?

STRATTON I don't know, Cole!

COLE They said they'd reschedule? Are you sure?

STRATTON That's what she, you know, Jack's umm –

COLE Thing, yeah –

STRATTON – Claire, that's what Claire said. But she's in bits, she was babbling, so who knows –

COLE What the fuck did Jack <u>do</u>, Stratt?

STRATTON Who can we call? Who do we know over the road?

COLE Jack, that's who we know over the road –

STRATTON Beth. Call Beth.

COLE Beth? What would Beth know?

STRATTON I thought she had a friend over there –

COLE Yeah, well –

STRATTON A friend in HR –

COLE Yeah, well, the thing is –

STRATTON If anyone knows anything, it'll be someone in HR –

COLE Thing is, I really don't want to call Beth –

STRATTON Why not? What's happened

COLE Nothing's <u>happened</u> –

STRATTON Cole, please, we, we need to, to –

COLE It's just a bit, you know, a bit wossername –

STRATTON Come on, we need the, the back story –

COLE Okay, okay, I'll call her, for fuck's sake –

STRATTON You call Beth, I'll call Frank.

COLE I'm calling her, alright?

> **COLE** *fingers his mobile.* **STRATTON** *dials his desk phone.*

STRATTON *(into phone)* It's Stratton, is he there?

    (...)

    Okay, I'll hold.

    Both waiting. Then:

COLE *(into phone)* Hey.

    (...)

    Yeah, yeah, okay, don't start –

    (...)

    No, I did not, I – hey, don't hang up! I – what?

    (...)

    No! The place was rammed, I went home didn't I?

    COLE *stands, walks as far away from* **STRATTON** *as possible.*

    (into phone) Oh really? You didn't look bored to me, doing shots with whatsisname –

    (...)

    No wait, that is so, you are so –

    (...)

    Well that's where you're wrong, isn't it, cos that's why I'm ringing...

STRATTON *(into phone)* Yes, I'm still here –

    (...)

    Well, it's important that I, that we –

    (...)

    No, no, no, I'll hold –

COLE *(into mobile)* Okay, okay –

    (lowering his voice)

    'Sorry'. Okay?

    (a little louder)

'Sorry', alright?

STRATTON *(into phone)* Yes? Good, good. Great. Thanks. Bye.

(hangs up)

Frank's popping down –

COLE So we're okay now, yeah?

(…)

Okay, sweet – hey, wait, did you hear about Jack Holland? Apparently he's –

(…)

Absolutely! He's gone! That's what we heard, so we're totally –

(…)

What?

STRATTON *gets up from his desk, walks over to* COLE.

He what?

(…)

Joking. <u>Joking</u> –

(…)

Wow.

STRATTON *hovers over* COLE, *trying to listen in.*

STRATTON What?

COLE *waves* STRATTON *away.*

COLE *(into phone)* No <u>way</u>!

STRATTON <u>What</u>?

COLE *(into phone)* It's Stratton, I'm in his office, we were just –

(…)

No, that's not why I rang –

(…)

– I rang to –

(…)

Will you just listen? I rang to –

(…)

Oh fuck off Beth –

(…)

Okay, you know what, I retract my apology –

(…)

<u>Retract</u>, look it up –

(as she hangs up on him)

Bitch! Fuck's sake!

STRATTON What? <u>What</u>?

COLE He was naked.

STRATTON <u>Jack</u>?

COLE Yes, <u>Jack!</u> They found him naked in a meeting room.

STRATTON Naked in a meeting room?

COLE That's what Beth heard. The room was trashed, he was raving apparently.

STRATTON <u>Raving</u>? <u>Jack</u>?

COLE Shouting and screaming, apparently –

STRATTON <u>Jack</u>? <u>Raving</u>?

COLE According to Beth. Bollock-naked, raving like a madman –

STRATTON No, no, Jack is one of the, Jack is about the sanest guy I know –

COLE I'm just saying, that's what they're saying –

STRATTON That's what Beth's saying –

COLE That's what Beth's mate over the road was saying –

STRATTON <u>Jack</u>? Ranting and raving?

COLE Waving his bits around –

The door right opens and **FRANK** – *fiftyish, impeccably suited and booted* – *enters.*

FRANK Put me out of my misery, gentlemen, I beg you. Take me out and shoot me –

> **FRANK** *collapses elegantly on the sofa next to* **COLE**, *puts his feet up on the table.*

STRATTON Frank, have you heard about Jack Holland?

FRANK Let me paint the picture. I'm in a meeting with a man, a man who has come to me with a proposal. Now this man is a rising star, he's not just flavour of the month – Cole, dear boy, do I have your attention?

– he's flavour of the year, of the decade even, so it behoves me to pay attention to his proposal which may shower us – you, me, this great organisation of ours – with untold riches, so there he is, proposing away, and there I am, listening away, but in fact – 'in reality' – I am looking at Mr Flavour's suit which is a perfectly respectable suit <u>in</u> <u>itself</u>: a single-breasted, three-button, dark blue worsted. A suit, in other words, which could cause no offence to anyone, but then I notice –

STRATTON Frank –

FRANK – <u>then</u> I notice his pocket handkerchief. Now I have no objection to the pocket handkerchief *per se,* but not – emphatically not – when it matches the tie –

COLE Oh my God.

FRANK Wait! When it matches the tie – <u>and</u> <u>the</u> <u>shirt</u>.

COLE Oh. My. God.

FRANK Suddenly my world is turned upside down, I am *completement bouleverse*, I am seeing Mr Flavour in an entirely new light. As I listen to his, his – Cole, what's that phrase that gives me cancer?

COLE 'Mission Statement'.

FRANK Exactly. As I listen to his, his 'thing', I find I can no longer take it seriously, I am now convinced that within it must lurk a failure of taste, a matching handkerchief as it were, a fatal flaw that renders it worthless, and despite the fact that I was unable to detect this flaw, I sent Mr Flavour packing. On what grounds? A sartorial indiscretion, nothing more. How will that play on the tenth floor, do you think, when I'm called to account for my actions? The man who turned down the Beatles, the man who turned down Microsoft!

COLE His handkerchief matched his tie, Frank –

FRANK – and his shirt!

COLE The man was a cunt, end of.

STRATTON Can we, can we just talk about the rather pressing matter of Jack Holland –

FRANK – ah, the matter of Jack –

STRATTON – because we should be sitting down with him now, this very minute, signing off on the, the –

FRANK – indeed you should –

COLE – Jack's gone –

STRATTON – security escorted Jack off the premises –

COLE – dragged him off bollock naked, screaming the odds –

FRANK – hush, children, you are getting overexcited –

STRATTON – but he has gone, hasn't he?

FRANK Yes, Jack has indeed gone.

STRATTON What did he do, Frank? What's the story?

FRANK Jack, as I understand it, was under a lot of pressure –

STRATTON – we're all under pressure, Frank, but Jack wasn't the kind to, to –

FRANK – marital pressure, Stratton.

STRATTON <u>Marital</u> pressure?

FRANK It transpires that his wife kicked him out –

STRATTON Sarah? <u>Sarah</u> kicked him out?

FRANK If 'Sarah' is his wife, then, yes, 'Sarah' kicked him out.

STRATTON But Jack is, is – I mean, his family is everything to him –

FRANK – but not he to them, it seems. He was given his marching orders. So he camped out in a meeting-room. Where he became a tad over-wrought. This did not go down well with the powers that be –

STRATTON – <u>Sarah</u> kicked him out? Why, for God's sake?

FRANK It seems he was conducting an inappropriate relationship –

COLE – he what?

FRANK – with a colleague –

COLE – no way! –

FRANK – which they tend to frown upon over the road –

STRATTON – but this, this is – Frank, are you sure about this?

FRANK I must emphasise, gentlemen, that it is completely unsubstantiated. Gossip, in other words, which of course we all deplore blah blah blah –

STRATTON Jack? <u>Jack</u>?

FRANK Stratton, please remove the look of stunned horror from your face, it's beginning to grate.

STRATTON But I've known Jack for years, and this is completely out of character –

COLE – the old perve.

FRANK I must admit, even I was mildly surprised, but please, can we not allow this shattering news to distract us from the matter in hand –

STRATTON's *mobile rings.*

STRATTON Sorry, sorry...

STRATTON *checks the number, answers it.*

Hi, hi, I'm – yes, I'm in a –

(...)

Okay, just, just –

STRATTON *makes an apologetic gesture to* **FRANK** *and* **COLE,** *and exits.*

FRANK Talk to me, Cole.

COLE Jack's gone? Best news in ages.

FRANK Really?

COLE Absolutely. We've been sitting here for weeks –

FRANK – months, actually –

COLE – sitting here for months, and round and round they go, Jack and Stratt, the licensing, the revenue stream, Asia for fuck's sake, round and round, doing my head in. Jack was risk averse, a classic jobsworth. Jack's gone? Hoofuckingray.

FRANK And Stratton?

COLE Getting worse. Micro-manages everything to death. And his wife, total nightmare, rings him five, ten times a day. We're in a meeting last week, she rings him, major crisis, her car's running out of petrol, she can't fill it, got a phobia about petrol pumps or something, he has to send Lucy, wife won't let Lucy drive her car without wearing surgical gloves, it's a fucking circus, Frank –

STRATTON *enters, talking into his mobile.*

STRATTON Open the cupboard and –

(…)

On the left, the switch on the left, darling. Alright?

(…)

Yes, I promise –

(…)

Okay, bye, bye.

(quiet)

Love you –

(…)

Bye.

(hangs up)

Sorry, sorry –

FRANK Stratton, Cole here was saying that Jack's unseemly exit may not be such a bad thing.

STRATTON How so?

COLE Look, Jack's gone, poor Jack, cry me a river, all I'm saying is, bottom line, now he's gone, maybe we can crack on, push this fucker through with someone else.

STRATTON Look, I've known Jack for years, I've been to his house –

COLE – oh please –

STRATTON No, listen Cole, there's got to be room in what we do for, for –

COLE For what, Stratt? Tell me.

STRATTON – some sort of mutual respect –

COLE – mutual bollocks, Stratt –

And **STRATTON**'s *desk phone rings. Silence for a beat. Then* **STRATTON** *goes to answer it.*

STRATTON *(into phone)* Yes, Lucy.

(…)

They said what?

(…)

Really?

(…)

<u>Tomorrow</u>? Are you sure?

(…)

Well, I – I – what's in the diary?

(…)

Okay, well I, I suppose that's okay, then –

(…)

Who? Say again? Hold on, let me, let me write that down…

STRATTON *looks in one inside pocket, then another. Then clicks his fingers, makes a writing gesture at* **FRANK** *and* **COLE**. **COLE** *shrugs – no pen.* **FRANK** *stands, takes out a pen, gives it to* **STRATTON**.

(into phone) Hold on, what was it again? Helen?

(…)

Helen…what? Davis? Okay –

(…)

Okay, thanks, Lucy.

(hangs up)

They've rescheduled. They're sending someone else. Tomorrow morning, ten-thirty.

FRANK *holds out a hand for his pen.* **STRATTON** *gives it to him.*

COLE Someone else? Who?

STRATTON A woman –

COLE A woman?

STRATTON Helen something –

Reading his note.

Helen Davis?

COLE Who the fuck is Helen Davis?

FRANK <u>Ellen</u>. Ellen David.

STRATTON You know this woman, Frank?

FRANK She's one of Jack's team –

COLE – great, a <u>minion</u> –

FRANK – she wrote the original report –

COLE They're sending a <u>minion</u>, it's bullshit bollocks while they re-group –

STRATTON – <u>she</u> wrote it? I thought Jack wrote it.

FRANK Jack doesn't write his reports any more than I do.

STRATTON But he never, he never mentioned her name –

FRANK Why would he? When Cole here pens one of his stream-of-consciousness rants, I brandish it at meetings as if it were my own – having rendered it into something approximating the English language.

STRATTON What's she like, Frank?

FRANK No idea, old sock –

COLE – time-wasting until they find someone to take over from Jack –

STRATTON Do they know about Jack on the tenth floor?

COLE – trying to keep us on-message –

FRANK – oh yes. They know.

STRATTON So what do they, I mean, how do we play this?

FRANK What was it you said, Cole? 'Crack on, push this fucker through?'

COLE Totally –

STRATTON But, but we don't know whether this woman, Helen –

FRANK Ellen –

STRATTON We don't know whether this 'Ellen' has the authority to, to sign off on the deal –

COLE She's an underling, Stratt!

FRANK Well, at ten-thirty tomorrow you'll find out, won't you? We must 'go with the flow', as my darling wife used to say.

STRATTON Maybe you should sit in on this one, Frank.

COLE Frank's not going to meet with a <u>minion</u>, is he?

FRANK We'll see. In the meantime, a gentle shot across your bows. You know I love you all, in my twisted way.

COLE Yeah, we're all loved up, Frank.

FRANK Except on the tenth floor, where they are not loved up at all, I'm afraid. In fact, alarm bells are ringing up there. They think that the abrupt and undignified manner of Jack Holland's departure means that our little project is about to go... Cole, what's that phrase that gives me cancer?

COLE 'Pear-shaped'.

FRANK Exactly. Let that not come to pass, I beg of you. Because if it does, I will cease to love you, the sky will fall in, and darkness will reign.

>   **FRANK** *exits. Silence as* **STRATTON** *and* **COLE** *reflect.*

COLE Shit.

>   *Beat.*

What was her name again?

STRATTON Ellen. Ellen David.

COLE Bitch on wheels. You wait and see.

>   *Blackout.*

TWO

The office the following morning.

STRATTON *enters, talking on his mobile. Sniffs the air, goes to the cupboard, sprays air freshener.*

STRATTON *(into phone)* Bleeding? <u>Bleeding</u>? My God –

(…)

You mean <u>profusely</u> or, or –

STRATTON *returns the air freshener to the cupboard.*

So, more of a graze, then –

(…)

No, I'm not trying to play it down, I'm just –

(…)

Well, where did she get the lighter from, that's the –

(…)

Okay, okay, but I've got this very important meeting, darling –

(…)

Yes, as soon as I come out of the meeting –

(…)

As soon as I come out of the –

(…)

As soon as I –

(…)

Okay. Okay. Give her my love, tell her Daddy is, is –

(…)

No, just say –

(…)

Okay, okay, I was just –

(…)

Okay, bye. Love you. Bye –

(…)

Bye.

(…)

Bye, bye.

STRATTON *hangs up, puts his mobile on the desk. Sticks a hand in an inside pocket, then remembers. He picks up his deskphone, punches in a number.*

(into phone) Lucy, any sign of my pen?

(…)

Did you look in the –

(…)

No? Okay, fine –

(…)

No, I looked everywhere at home –

(…)

Don't worry, I'm sure it will turn up –

(…)

No, don't! Seriously, Lucy, it's not the cleaner, absolutely not, Mblele would never –

(…)

Well, I don't agree and anyway, I don't want to go down that road, really. I'm sure it will turn up –

(…)

Okay, great, thanks Lucy.

STRATTON *hangs up, goes to the sofas and low table, starts straightening magazines, arranging glasses, water etc.*

Enter COLE.

COLE Hey, Stratt, guess what? Unfuckingbelievable. I was in Treats last night with Beth and her mate –

STRATTON I was thinking I should sit here –

COLE Guess what she told us –

COLE *sits, gets his laptop out of his bag.*

STRATTON No, no, you sit here –

STRATTON *indicates the end of the other sofa.*

COLE Stratt, you've got to listen to this –

COLE *moves.*

STRATTON – and I'll sit here –

STRATTON *sits at the other end of the same sofa as* COLE.

COLE – it's unfuckingbelievable –

STRATTON – and she can sit there –

COLE Stratt!

STRATTON *indicates the empty sofa.*

STRATTON – maybe that's a little intimidating. Better if I sit here –

COLE It was her!

STRATTON *moves to the empty sofa.*

STRATTON – then she can sit there –

STRATTON *indicates the angle where the sofas meet, i.e. between the two men.*

COLE It was her, Stratt!

STRATTON Who, Beth? What about her?

COLE No, no, whatsername. <u>Helen</u>.

STRATTON What about her?

COLE It was her. It was her Jack was having a thing with. His 'inappropriate relationship', Stratt! It was her! Wossername, Helen!

STRATTON Beth told you this?

COLE Beth's mate! It started on some bonding weekend – you know, get your team over the river with a piece of string and a plank. Beth's mate was there.

STRATTON Beth's mate?

COLE Beth's mate in HR over the road. She was there for some of it, anyway.

STRATTON Her <u>mate</u>?

COLE Yeah. Or Beth's mate's mate, I dunno, whatever, anyway she was in the same group as Jack and wossername –

STRATTON Beth's mate's mate – ?

COLE – yeah, and she says wossername was shagging Jack cross-eyed –

STRATTON Beth's mate's mate was shagging Jack?

COLE No! Keep up, Stratt, fuck's sake! This Helen was shagging him, shagging him like he's never been shagged before, epic sex, Jack's cross-eyed with it, he loses the plot completely, goes home one night, tells the wife he's 'in love', guess what, the wife kicks him out – then, wait for it, wossername, <u>Helen,</u> knocks him back, she's had second thoughts right, he's a married man, it'll never work blah blah, thanks for the memories, we'll always have Paris, bosh, poor old Jack is now truly fucked – goodbye marriage, goodbye house, hallo lawyers and, insult to injury, no more epic shagging. Cue music –

STRATTON – this is just, this is just –

COLE – no wonder poor old Jack goes ape in a meeting-room –

STRATTON – this is just gossip, and anyway –

The phone on **STRATTON***'s desk rings.* **STRATTON** *gets up, goes to answer it.*

(into phone) Yes, Lucy.

To **COLE**.

She's here.

COLE Tell her to wait.

STRATTON *(into phone)* Ask her to wait, please Lucy. Thank you.

(hangs up)

It's hearsay and anyway, it's none of our business and –

COLE Listen, Beth's mate says two years ago this Helen was <u>temping</u> for Jack, next thing she writing his reports, now she's taking his fucking meetings! What did I tell you, Stratt? A piece of work, a bitch on wheels –

As he talks, **COLE** *takes his coat off, flings it on one of the sofas along with his bag, adds magazines from the table until there's only a small space left at the upstage end of the sofa.*

STRATTON – and even if it's true, it has no bearing on this meeting –

COLE – so she can sit here –

COLE *indicates the small space left at the end of one sofa.*

– and we'll sit here because, and excuse me for stating the obvious Stratt, but the whole fucking point is to intimidate her!

STRATTON Cole, this is a meet-and-greet –

COLE Absolutely. Totally. I can't wait to meet-and-greet this bitch.

STRATTON – and I don't want it to be confrontational –

COLE I'm saying nothing, mate.

STRATTON *goes to his desk, picks up his phone, punches a number.*

STRATTON Seriously, Cole.

COLE Not a word.

STRATTON *(into phone)* Show her in, please Lucy.

COLE Totally stumm –

The door opens and **ELLEN** *David stands on the threshold. 30's, soberly dressed. She's carrying a laptop bag and wearing a laminated visitors' badge.*

STRATTON Ellen, come in. I'm Stratton –

STRATTON *extends his hand.* **ELLEN** *shakes it.*

Good to meet you.

ELLEN And you. I've heard a lot about you.

STRATTON *guides her towards the sofas.*

STRATTON And this is Cole.

COLE *nods without looking up from his laptop.*

ELLEN Hallo.

STRATTON Take a seat, please.

> **STRATTON** *indicates the small space at the end of the sofa strewn with stuff but* **ELLEN** *sits on the same sofa as* **COLE**. **COLE** *looks up from his laptop.* **ELLEN** *smiles at him, gets out her laptop.* **COLE** *moves further away from her.*

> **STRATTON** *clears a space for himself, sits at the end of the other sofa.*

Ellen, can I get you anything?

Coffee? Tea?

ELLEN No, thank you –

COLE So what's the story with old Jack then?

STRATTON Cole, let's not –

COLE I'm only asking –

ELLEN No, no, I quite understand –

COLE – I'm only asking because we've been working with old Jack for months, and suddenly, bosh, old Jack's gone 'cause he was bollock naked in a meeting-room –

ELLEN Well, that's not quite –

COLE 'Allegedly' –

STRATTON What Cole's trying to say is –

ELLEN It's alright, really. It's been a very difficult time for all of us –

STRATTON Of course, of course –

ELLEN – but for legal reasons I can't discuss Mr Holland's current situation –

COLE What's to discuss? Jack's gone.

ELLEN Actually, he's on sick leave, indefinite sick leave, and there's every possibility that Mr Holland will return to work at some time in the future –

COLE – joking –

ELLEN – and of course we wish him well in that respect –

STRATTON – as do we, as do we –

ELLEN – and that really is all I can say about the matter, I'm afraid.

STRATTON Well, I've been working with Jack for some time now and during that time, Jack has become a valued colleague and friend, so this is a genuine, a genuine blow, business aside of course –

ELLEN Of course –

STRATTON – and if there's some way you could pass on our best wishes to Jack –

ELLEN Well, there are legal restraints which prevent me – us, that's to say any employees of the company, from communicating with Mr Holland. And he with us, of course –

STRATTON Of course –

ELLEN But that's contractual, nothing should be read into it –

STRATTON Absolutely not.

> *Silence.* **ELLEN** *crosses her legs, sits back.* **COLE** *hunches over his keyboard. Stabs at a key.*

STRATTON Would you like some water? There's still or sparkling.

ELLEN No, thank you. I'm fine.

COLE *(not looking at her)* Okay, look – Helen, right? – can we move on please Helen and get a couple of things sorted?

ELLEN Of course. But first, can I just say we're still absolutely committed to this deal?

STRATTON Well, that's good to hear –

ELLEN Subject, of course, to all the elements being in place –

COLE They are in place, that's the thing, that's what we've been doing here –

STRATTON – Jack was very happy, we were all very happy with the final agreement –

COLE – what we've been doing, with Jack, is getting the elements in place, and yesterday, right, we were going to sign off, Jack was going to sign off on the deal, end of story, cue music –

STRATTON Yes, that's pretty much where we're at – ready to sign off on the deal –

COLE You see, what I, what we want to know is, can you?

STRATTON Cole, it's perhaps a little early to –

COLE I just want to know, Stratt – can she?

ELLEN Can I what?

COLE Can you sign off on the deal? Because if you can't, what we need, no disrespect Helen, is to be in the room with someone who can.

ELLEN I take your point, but the problem is, Mr Holland didn't keep me in the loop regarding the negotiations.

COLE Okay, so what we need, you see, is to be in the room with someone who <u>was</u> in the loop <u>and</u> can sign off on the deal –

ELLEN The problem is, Mr Holland didn't keep anyone in the loop.

Beat.

STRATTON We'd – we'd be happy to talk you through the whole thing, show you the projections, the research –

COLE Can you sign off the deal, Helen?

ELLEN I'll need to familarise myself with –

COLE Can you?

Pause.

ELLEN Yes, I can.

Beat.

And it's <u>Ellen</u>.

COLE That's what I said.

ELLEN Did you? I'm sorry.

STRATTON This is, this is excellent. As I said, we would be very happy to take you through the contract step–by-step–

ELLEN Thank you, that would be very helpful.

STRATTON In fact we could crack on immediately –

ELLEN Unfortunately I've got meetings for the rest of the day –

STRATTON Well, whenever you, you –

ELLEN Tomorrow would be good –

STRATTON Absolutely, let's pencil in tomorrow –

ELLEN In the meantime, perhaps you could email me the draft contract as it stands so I can look it over.

STRATTON You mean you haven't read the latest draft?

ELLEN No, I haven't.

STRATTON But surely your legal people have seen it –

ELLEN Mr Holland hadn't communicated with the legal department for some weeks. Or anyone else for that matter.

COLE Perhaps he had something else on his mind.

ELLEN Well, he was – <u>is</u> a very busy man.

   COLE *laughs.*

STRATTON But surely it's on his, his…

COLE – database?

ELLEN It seems it was inadvertently deleted.

COLE 'Inadvertently'!

ELLEN There have been problems with the new system. Which is why, in view of the time-frame, the sooner we can see what's in the contract the better.

STRATTON Of course, absolutely –

COLE 'Time-frame'? What 'time-frame'?

ELLEN I don't think this should necessarily be a problem, but the option runs out in…

   ELLEN *hits a key on her laptop.*

   …in two working days, i.e. tomorrow.

COLE The option? The <u>option</u>?

   COLE *gets to his feet, agitated.*

   The <u>option</u> runs out?

ELLEN But you knew that –

COLE Of course I knew that! But it was not an issue! Because – excuse me for pointing out the glaringly obvious – because we were going to sign off on it yesterday. Therefore it was not an issue. You see what I'm saying? It was not an issue. And now you're saying it's an issue.

ELLEN I didn't say it was an issue. In fact, I said it shouldn't be a problem –

STRATTON – of course not. But it's something we have to keep in mind –

ELLEN – exactly –

STRATTON – in fact it may only serve to keep us focussed –

ELLEN That's a very useful way of looking at it, Stratton.

STRATTON Thank you.

The door opens and **FRANK** *enters.*

FRANK Forgive me for intruding, people –

FRANK *goes over to* **ELLEN** *and extends a hand.*

You must be Ellen David. Frank Hanson.

ELLEN Hallo.

They shake hands.

FRANK Thought I'd drop in, see how things were progressing down at the coal face. And of course to say how sorry I am to hear about Jack Holland. Jack's a good man, I'm sure he'll be back amongst us in no time.

ELLEN Yes, I'm sure he will.

FRANK So. How <u>are</u> things progressing?

STRATTON Frank, we were, we were discussing a slight anomaly –

FRANK An 'anomaly'. Oh dear.

FRANK *smiles at* **ELLEN**. *She smiles back.*

STRATTON Well, not so much an anomaly as a, a –

COLE – fuck-up.

FRANK Well, that's what 'anomalies' often turn out to be, in my experience.

STRATTON Jack's data has, has been lost –

COLE 'Inadvertently' –

STRATTON – so we must bring Ellen up to speed, obviously, before she can sign off on the deal.

FRANK Well, of course we must. And we must bear in mind that the option runs out in –

To ELLEN.

– two working days?

ELLEN Yes.

FRANK Tomorrow, in fact.

STRATTON Yes, the option, exactly –

FRANK Well, this should only serve to concentrate our minds, shouldn't it?

STRATTON That's exactly what I, what we were saying –

ELLEN – yes, that's exactly what Stratton was saying –

FRANK – and hopefully your legal people will expedite matters.

ELLEN Well, lawyers, you know what they're like, they don't always see the big picture –

FRANK – so true –

STRATTON – yes, yes, absolutely –

ELLEN – and sometimes they forget that they are working for us instead of the other way round –

FRANK – <u>so</u> true –

STRATTON – absolutely –

ELLEN – but I'm a lawyer myself, and I have some experience with these contracts, so that should speed things up.

A beat as they digest this. Then FRANK *and* STRATTON *start talking simultaneously.*

FRANK/STRATTON. Well, that's marvellous –/That's, that's, that's –

FRANK – very good news, excellent news –

STRATTON Excellent news indeed.

To **FRANK**.

Ellen has to go to another meeting, so we're pencilling in tomorrow.

To **ELLEN**.

Shall we say ten-thirty?

ELLEN That should be fine. I'll get Claire to check my diary and call – it's Lucy, isn't it?

STRATTON Lucy, absolutely –

ELLEN – to call Lucy and confirm.

To **FRANK**.

As you can imagine, things are a little frantic over the road.

FRANK Yes, I can imagine.

ELLEN stands, **STRATTON** *follows suit with alacrity.* **COLE** *remains seated, hunched over his laptop.*

ELLEN extends her hand to **STRATTON***, who shakes it.*

ELLEN And you'll email me the draft contract.

STRATTON Right away.

FRANK Kiss of death to say it, Ellen, but I've got a very good feeling about this.

ELLEN shakes hands with **FRANK***.*

ELLEN Me too.

ELLEN turns to **COLE** *who's on his laptop.*

Good to have met you, Cole.

COLE *(not looking up)* Yeah, okay.

ELLEN I'll see you both tomorrow then.

No response from **COLE**.

STRATTON We look forward to it –

> **STRATTON** *escorts* **ELLEN** *to the door, opens it.*

ELLEN Thank you. Goodbye.

FRANK Goodbye.

STRATTON Bye. See you tomorrow. Bye…

> **ELLEN** *exits and* **STRATTON** *closes the door. A moment as they reflect.*

Well? Frank?

> **FRANK** *doesn't answer.*

COLE Nightmare. 'I'll get Claire to check my diary!' Purleease! She hasn't got a fucking diary, Jack's only been gone five minutes –

STRATTON What do you think, Frank?

> **FRANK** *doesn't answer.*

COLE 'Subject to all the elements being in place'. Bitch on fucking wheels, mate! And since when was the option an issue?

FRANK The option has always been an issue.

COLE Do what?

FRANK The option has always been an issue.

STRATTON Well, it's always been there, yes –

COLE Always 'been there'? What are you talking about, Stratt?

STRATTON Well, you know, the time factor has always been a, a factor –

COLE You're joking me! The 'time factor?' With you and Jack fannying around like a pair of old women, arguing this, arguing that, arguing the kitchen fucking sink, and now you give me '<u>time</u> factor'!

STRATTON Yes, well –

FRANK Alright, Stratton. Allow me.

Beat.

The feeling was that we might suggest, late in the day, a couple of amendments, apparently innocuous amendments, Cole, which contained – how can I put this? – the <u>tiniest</u> of traps, and dear old Jack, in his eagerness to sign off the deal, would accept them.

Silence.

COLE You were letting the clock run down.

STRATTON Well, in a sense, I suppose you could say –

COLE And you didn't tell me about this?

STRATTON Cole, there's a sense in which –

COLE Yeah, there's a sense in which you can both go and fuck yourselves! You didn't <u>tell</u> me?

FRANK It wasn't necessary, Cole. In fact it was preferable. Your natural impatience gave proceedings an admirable credibility.

COLE All that time without telling me. How's that supposed to make me feel?

FRANK Dear boy, we were only trying to protect you from the nasty machinations of the grown-ups.

COLE Last minute amendments?

FRANK Tiny, <u>tiny</u> amendments, Cole. And tucked away inside them, a delicious little trap devised, camouflaged and curlicued by Stratton in his inimitable way.

COLE Okay, okay, we can still do it, can't we? This is even better for us, isn't it? She doesn't know if she's coming or going, we nail her, she's gets her little pen out last thing tomorrow, bosh, we hit her with the amendments –

STRATTON I don't know, Cole –

COLE Come on, they're gagging for it, aren't they?

STRATTON Well, I'm not sure about that –

COLE Come on, they want the deal!

STRATTON <u>Jack</u> wanted the deal –

COLE – <u>they</u> want the deal!

FRANK Not the same thing.

COLE What? What?

STRATTON You heard what she said. Jack wasn't talking to anybody over there –

FRANK – because he was afraid they'd pull the plug on him. <u>He</u> liked the deal, <u>they</u> didn't. The fact is, dear Jack was on the slide which we thought was to our advantage. It's a matter of perception, Cole –

STRATTON Yes, that's it. The way things are, are perceived –

COLE I understand perception. You don't have to lecture me about perception –

FRANK – the perception was that they wanted the deal more than us. The perception <u>now</u> may be that we want the deal more than them.

COLE More than <u>her</u>, you mean.

FRANK Yes, Ms. David may well be in the driving-seat. The question is, does she know it?

COLE Course she does, bitch on fucking wheels –

STRATTON Cole, will you please, I'm sorry, but will you please stop it?

COLE Stop what?

STRATTON The language, the – the verbal abuse, it's not helpful. She's trying to do her job, like us, and I thought she handled it very well –

COLE You are such a push-over, Stratt, it's tragic.

STRATTON What, what are you saying, exactly –

COLE She does eye contact, smiles, uses your name – 'That's a <u>very</u> useful way of looking at it, Stratton' – and next thing you're bending over, arse in the air, 'Do me now!' –

STRATTON No, no, that's – that's –

COLE – which is no doubt how she mullered poor old Jack –

STRATTON No Cole, you can't, you can't –

FRANK Wait. 'How she 'mullered' poor old Jack'? Translate, please.

COLE It was her! Jack's 'inappropriate relationship! It was the bitch on wheels!

FRANK And this information comes from where?

STRATTON Gossip, Frank, tittle-tattle –

COLE Beth. Beth's mate –

STRATTON Beth's mate's mate –

COLE Whatever! Who cares? It's true! She was doing a number on us, Stratt! Come on, you saw the way she waltzed in here, parked her fat arse practically on top of me, invading my space, nerve of the woman. Crossing her legs in her fuck-me fucking shoes –

STRATTON Crossing her, her – ?

COLE – crossing them, uncrossing them, waving them all over the shop, she was coming on to me. You too, Stratt.

STRATTON Coming on to me?

*And **STRATTON**'s mobile rings.*

No Cole, seriously, you're way off the, the –

STRATTON *answers his mobile.*

(into phone) Hallo?

(…)

Hold on, darling, hold on –

(…)

Yes, it's over but –

(…)

Okay, okay, hold on –

To the others.

One minute…

STRATTON *gestures apologetically and exits.*

COLE The oven's on fire. The cat's stuck in the catflap –

FRANK Talking of Beth.

COLE We weren't.

FRANK We are now.

COLE Why?

FRANK Unlike our friends over the road, we take a liberal view on these matters.

COLE What matters?

FRANK Colleagues who see each other out of office hours. Who engage in 'social interaction not directly related to the workplace'. The view is that it's none of our business as long as it doesn't – I can scarcely bring myself to say this – as long as it doesn't 'impact on good working practice'.

COLE Yeah well, me and Beth…

FRANK Yes?

COLE I knocked it on the head.

FRANK Really?

COLE End of. Cue music.

FRANK Is that what last night's tantrum in Treats was all about?

COLE She threw a wobbly, didn't she? Silly bitch.

FRANK From what I hear, the wobbly was thrown by you.

COLE What? Who told you that?

FRANK Strange choice of venue to effect a *rapprochement* with one's girlfriend—

COLE yeah, well –

FRANK – a bar where naked Eastern Europeans cavort in gloomy booths –

COLE – it's a laugh, Frank, it's jokes. You wouldn't get it.

FRANK Hopefully not, but I believe Beth has become rather fond of the place.

COLE She goes there with me. For a laugh. Why?

FRANK There are rumours about Beth on the tenth floor.

COLE What rumours?

FRANK One does not want to be the subject of rumours on the tenth floor. You might mention it next time you see her –

COLE What rumours? Come on, Frank, what's the story?

FRANK I have no idea Cole, and frankly, I couldn't care less.

I simply mention, in passing, as a friend, that there are murmurs on the tenth floor about your raggle–taggle chum in the ever-so-slightly too short skirts –

STRATTON *enters, on his mobile.*

STRATTON *(into mobile)* Okay, okay. Now I really must –

(…)

Okay. Bye –

(…)

Yes, bye –

(…)

You too. Bye. Bye –

(…)

Bye.

STRATTON *hangs up.*

Sorry, sorry.

FRANK As I was saying. In my view there is no point in trying to second–guess Ms. David. For what it's worth, I think she will take this to the wire. In which case we'll stick to the strategy devised for dear old Jack.

COLE She's going to rub our noses in it and she's going to love every minute.

FRANK I suspect you're right, but we must grin and bear it. Tomorrow therefore, all will be sweetness and light. Eat a decent breakfast at home, break early for lunch, send out for sandwiches. Make the afternoon a long one. Be pedantic, spare her no detail. Let blood sugar levels plummet. Then I will arrive with the amendments. I will be apologetic – 'It's the tenth floor, completely out of my hands' – but brisk. I will offer to go over the amendments with her. On the surface, they are utterly straightforward. Will she want to confer with her colleagues over the road?

Possibly, but my instinct tells me no. She will lose face if she has to seek advice on such plain fare.

Ms. David, it seems to me, is not a woman who likes to lose face. Will she sign? Maybe, maybe not, who knows? Let the cards fall where they may, we will have done all that we can.

Beat.

And now, Cole, if you don't mind, I want a word with Stratton.

COLE Frank, can I talk to you –

FRANK No, you can't.

COLE Frank –

FRANK Bugger off, there's a good boy.

Exit **COLE**, *already thumbing his phone.*

Everything alright at home, old sock?

STRATTON Yes, yes, fine. Mostly fine.

Beat.

Well, actually, not entirely, no.

FRANK Oh dear.

STRATTON There is a slight, there is a cloud or two on the horizon as it happens.

FRANK As what happens?

STRATTON Well... Claudia has an, an aggressive streak, you see, she gets into fights –

FRANK My God. Did you know this when you married her?

STRATTON No, Claudia is my daughter –

FRANK – of course she is, <u>Claudia</u>, yes –

STRATTON – and we've been seeing a counsellor, and things do seem to be improving –

FRANK I'm sure it's just a phase, Stratton. Hormonal, perhaps.

STRATTON – but Vanessa is having, well, trouble coping with the, the –

FRANK Vanessa?

STRATTON My wife –

FRANK <u>Vanessa</u>, of course, forgive me –

STRATTON – Vanessa is having trouble coping with the, you know, the whole situation and she, well, she's an emotional woman, there are issues, you see –

FRANK 'Issues'? Oh dear.

STRATTON – but you know, apart from that, things are pretty good, a lot to be positive about –

FRANK Well, as my darling wife used to say, fate plays us for a fool, doesn't she? I could weep sometimes – no, that's going too far, I couldn't <u>weep</u> to be honest, if only I could, but anyway, listen, the thing is, the wife's not the full shilling, the daughter's a psychopath, and I feel your pain Stratton, I really do, but I must ask you, when I'm in your office and, more importantly, when Ms David is in your office, will you turn your fucking phone off!

Silence. Eventually:

STRATTON It isn't going to work, Frank.

FRANK What?

STRATTON Hitting Ellen David with last minute amendments. She'll be suspicious. Who wouldn't be? Last minute amendments to the Secondary Licensing? She'll take the amendments apart comma by comma, and if she's smart, which I think she is, she'll find the trap.

FRANK So what do you suggest?

> **STRATTON** *doesn't respond.*

> Stratton, please don't make me threaten you, you know how it upsets me.

STRATTON Put the amendments in the draft contract now, before we send it to her. They've only got twenty-four hours to go through it. They may miss the trap.

FRANK And if they don't? What if she turns up tomorrow and queries it?

STRATTON We give her more amendments.

FRANK <u>More</u> amendments? What do you mean?

> **STRATTON** *doesn't answer.*

> TALK TO ME, STRATTON!

> *Blackout.*

THREE

The office the following morning.

COLE, *agitated, is pacing around, texting on his mobile. Presses 'send' emphatically, sits on one of the sofas, puts his phone down, stares at it. Picks it up almost immediately. Stands, paces, texts, presses 'send'. Puts phone in pocket, sits. Takes phone out, stares at it. Stands again, starts texting and pacing.*

STRATTON *comes in, talking on his phone.* STRATTON *and* COLE *dodge ineptly round each other –* STRATTON *talking,* COLE *texting – as* STRATTON *makes his way to his desk.*

STRATTON *(into mobile)* No, I'm there, I mean I'm here, I've just walked in –

(…)

STRATTON *freezes.*

(into phone) What? In the mouth?

(…)

She had a, a – ?

(…)

A garlic press? What was she doing with a – a – ?

(…)

Yes, 'show and tell', I understand, but a, a garlic –

(…)

But he is conscious –

(…)

Thank God, but – what?

(…)

I am a little concerned about Toby's teeth actually. How many did she –

(…)

Alright, alright –

(…)

Darling, I told you I'll be in a meeting until lunchtime, I have to turn my phone off –

(…)

I know –

(…)

I know –

(…)

Yes. You too. Bye, bye –

(…)

Of course I do. Bye, bye.

(…)

Bye.

(…)

Bye.

> **STRATTON** *hangs up, sniffs the air.*

COLE Stratt, can I ask you something?

> **STRATTON** *takes the air freshener out of the cupboard, sprays it around.*

You know Beth?

STRATTON Beth?

COLE Yeah, <u>Beth</u> –

STRATTON What about her – wait, isn't she on the fourth
floor? Because there's security all over the place down
there, there's been a break-in or something –

COLE Have you heard anything about her? You know,
<u>rumours</u>.

STRATTON Rumours? What rumours?

COLE About <u>Beth</u> –

STRATTON Rumours about <u>Beth</u>?

COLE Frank said they were talking about her on the tenth
floor. I just wondered if you'd heard anything.

STRATTON No, no, nothing. What kind of rumours?
Rumours relating to what?

COLE It doesn't matter…

STRATTON *(checks watch)* Okay, right, the meeting. Cole?
This is what we'll do. If she sits here, where she was
yesterday, I'll sit here, beside her, because I'll be doing
most of the talking, and you, you sit here, next to me
but to one side. And it's the usual routine, okay? I deal
with specifics, you only talk if she has concerns about
the bigger picture, and Cole, please, could you, could
you dial down the, the – could you be, you know,
<u>amiable</u>?

COLE Rumours relating to: is she seeing anyone in the
building, that's what.

STRATTON Sorry?

COLE <u>Beth</u>. Who's she shagging, Stratt, that's what I want
to know –

STRATTON Well, I – I – how would I know?

COLE They're talking about her on the tenth floor.

STRATTON Cole, I'm, I'm –

COLE Frank might have said something to you.

STRATTON About Beth? Why – why would he? We don't, we don't talk about that sort of –

COLE Maybe it's someone on the tenth floor. Maybe she's shagging someone on the tenth floor.

STRATTON Someone on the tenth floor? That seems, that seems highly –

COLE You know what? It's my fault, Stratt. When I met her she didn't know her arse from her elbow, but I took her to Treats, I let the genie out of the, the wossername –

STRATTON – the bottle –

COLE – and now she's totally out of control –

STRATTON – but I thought you and Beth were – the thing is, Cole, I can't keep up, are you together or not?

COLE Yes. No. Does it matter? They're talking about her on the tenth floor, which means they're talking about <u>me</u>! Jesus, Stratt, don't you get it?

STRATTON Cole, are you alright?

COLE I'm good, I'm great –

STRATTON No, seriously, are you? Because if you're not, maybe you should go home, let me deal with this –

COLE Oh no, you're not rowing me out of this, this is my baby –

STRATTON I know that, Cole –

COLE – my idea –

STRATTON – I know, I'm just saying, if you're, if you're upset –

COLE Fuck's sake, I'm fine –

STRATTON Because this has got to work, Cole, you heard what Frank said –

COLE I just want to know what they're saying about me on the –

STRATTON Will you please for once LISTEN TO ME?!

Silence.

Look, Frank as good as spelled it out yesterday and I daresay you weren't listening as usual but we – you, me, Frank – we're hanging on by our fingernails here and if we don't push this through, they're going to shut us down, this department is gone, we're gone. Well, I've got a family, I've got a wife who elects not to work, a decision I wholeheartedly support by the way, I have schooling and, and a mortgage, and overheads, many, many overheads, and what I want to say to you, Cole, with all due respect, is I am not going to let you sabotage this meeting, my meeting, because your ex-girlfriend is having sex with somebody else in the building.

Beat.

Your ex-girlfriend who, hitherto, you have treated with utter contempt.

Beat.

From what little I have observed.

Beat.

I'm sorry, but –

The phone on **STRATTON**'s *desk rings.* **STRATTON** *is still holding the air freshener. He puts it down on the desk and answers the phone.*

(*into phone*) Hallo.

(…)

One second, Lucy.

STRATTON *covers the mouthpiece.*

(to **COLE***)* She's here. Are we, are we okay?

Beat.

Cole?

COLE *finally nods.*

(into phone) Ask her to come in please, Lucy.

STRATTON *hangs up the phone, goes to the door, opens it.* **ELLEN** *is standing there.*

Ellen, come in.

ELLEN Thanks.

STRATTON Sit down, please.

STRATTON *ushers* **ELLEN** *to the sofas.*

ELLEN Thank you –

To **COLE**.

Hallo.

COLE *gives her a minimal nod.*

Sorry I'm a little late. Your security people are being very thorough today.

Without prompting, **ELLEN** *sits where she sat previously.* **STRATTON** *sits opposite her.*

STRATTON Oh God, sorry about that, there's been some sort of problem on the fourth floor –

At this point, **COLE** *is still on his feet.*

Cole?

COLE *sits where* STRATTON *previously indicated. All three deploy their laptops.*

Can I get you anything? Coffee? Tea?

ELLEN No, I'm fine thanks.

STRATTON Help yourself to water if you…

ELLEN Thank you.

STRATTON So, so how do you want to do this? Shall I start from the top –

ELLEN No, that won't be necessary, Stratton. I only have a couple of queries –

STRATTON Great, excellent –

COLE So everyone's in the loop now, are they?

ELLEN I'm sorry?

COLE Your lot. Over the road. You were saying yesterday that Jack hadn't kept anyone in the loop.

ELLEN Yes, everyone's well and truly in the loop now.

STRATTON Excellent. Very good.

ELLEN Shall I kick off then?

No response from **COLE**.

STRATTON Yes, absolutely.

ELLEN *turns to her laptop and hits a key.*

ELLEN Okay, my first query is just a question of phrasing, really.

STRATTON Phrasing?

ELLEN Yes. The clause in question is on page –

And the phone on **STRATTON**'s *desk rings.*

STRATTON Sorry, sorry –

STRATTON *gets up and goes to his desk, picks up the phone.*

Lucy, I'm in the middle of – what?

(…)

What, now? Really?

(…)

But I've got Ellen David here and we're just –

(…)

Alright. Okay, tell them I'm on my way.

STRATTON *hangs up.*

Look, I'm really sorry. Heads of Department have been called in, it's about this break-in on the fourth floor. It'll only take five minutes.

ELLEN *(checks her watch)* Well, I was hoping we could get through this as quickly as possible.

STRATTON Five, ten minutes maximum, I promise.

ELLEN Okay, not a problem.

STRATTON Anything you want, just ask Lucy.

ELLEN Thank you.

Beat.

STRATTON Alright, Cole?

COLE Yeah.

STRATTON *goes to the door, pauses. Reluctant to go.*

STRATTON Cole?

COLE What?

STRATTON Nothing.

STRATTON *exits.* COLE *picks up his phone, starts texting.*

ELLEN So. This looks very promising.

No response from COLE *who's texting furiously.*

Don't you think?

COLE Yeah, it's sweet.

ELLEN *hits a key on her laptop.*

ELLEN The only real problem I have is with the Secondary Licensing clause.

COLE *(texting)* You'll have to wait until Stratt gets back. I don't do clauses.

ELLEN Alright.

ELLEN *sits back, crosses her legs.* COLE *jumps to his feet, moves away. Presses 'send'.*

You're the ideas man, right?

COLE Something like that.

ELLEN Leave the nuts and bolts to others.

COLE Yeah, sort of thing.

ELLEN Making the entry-level kit free of charge, that was you, was it?

COLE Yeah.

ELLEN Very, very clever.

COLE Yeah, well.

COLE *sits, looks at his phone, then chucks it down on the table, frustrated at the lack of response.*

You know what pisses me off?

ELLEN No, I don't.

COLE Mysteries.

ELLEN What kind of mysteries?

COLE When people won't tell you what's going on.

Beat.

You know what I think?

ELLEN No, I don't.

COLE It's worse than lying.

ELLEN How?

COLE Someone <u>lies</u> to you, at least they're making an effort.

ELLEN That's…interesting.

COLE Well, I'm an interesting guy, Helen.

ELLEN Ellen.

COLE That's what I said.

Silence.

ELLEN I think I know what this is about.

COLE You do?

> **ELLEN** *uncrosses her legs, leans forward and opens a bottle of mineral water. Pours herself a glass, holds up the bottle to* **COLE** *who shakes his head.* **ELLEN** *has a drink, puts the glass down, crosses her legs and sits back.*

ELLEN There's a problem, isn't there? Here. Between us.

> **COLE** *doesn't answer.*

Isn't there, Cole?

COLE Maybe.

ELLEN Yes. And it's to do with Jack Holland. Someone you worked closely with. Someone you trusted. Someone who became a friend. Now he's gone. And you think I'm...implicated.

Beat.

So, in the interests of peace, goodwill and future... good relations, I'm going to tell you a story.

COLE A story. Excellent.

ELLEN But it's not about me and Jack. It's important you understand that.

COLE Yeah, I get it.

ELLEN Okay...

> **ELLEN** *uncrosses her legs, takes a drink of water. Stands, walks a few feet, turns to face* **COLE**. *She will pace, on and off, during the following:*

...a woman gets a new job. New job, new boss. The new boss is an intelligent, hard-working man. He's good at his job, and so's she. He encourages her, gives her lots of responsibility. They work well together. They put in long hours. There are trips.

Beat.

There are moments, obviously. Their hands brush when he passes her a document. Their heads touch as they lean over a laptop on a plane. Once, getting out of a taxi, the woman stumbles and her boss grabs her arm to steady her. These moments, they don't <u>mean</u> anything.

COLE 'Course they don't.

ELLEN Meanwhile, on the domestic front...things aren't going too well with the woman and her partner.

COLE Why's that then?

ELLEN Take a guess.

COLE Umm...she's working too hard?

ELLEN Yes. And there's something else. What's the really bad thing she's doing?

COLE Ummm...she earns more than him?

ELLEN *laughs.*

ELLEN Yes! She's more <u>successful</u>.

COLE Bad girl.

ELLEN Bad, bad girl.

Beat.

So they split. It's messy.

COLE Money. The mortgage.

ELLEN The espresso machine, everything.

Beat.

Then, one weekend, there's a conference.

COLE Right. The country hotel. The team-building.

ELLEN No, a conference. The Chinese, the Germans. It's hard work.

COLE Course it is.

ELLEN Afterwards, the woman and her boss go for a drink. They drink more than usual. Suddenly, somehow or other, she's telling him about the change in her circumstances. Matter-of-fact. Business-like. A wry joke here and there. But the woman's boss is upset. This is terrible, he says, I'm so sorry. Are you alright? She reassures him, she's <u>fine</u>. 'Are you sure?'. Yes, <u>fine</u>. Really. Then he puts his hand over hers –

Whoah –

ELLEN – but only for a second. Then the moment is over. And the evening progresses without incident. They part as usual. An air kiss on the pavement, a taxi for her, a taxi for him…

COLE Go on then.

ELLEN It's the weekend after the conference. Sunday evening. She gets a text from him. He's never contacted her on a Sunday before. He's scrupulous about such things.

Beat.

The text says 'Are you alright?' She ignores it. An hour later, another: 'Is everything alright? I'm concerned'. She eventually replies: 'I'm fine. Goodnight'. An hour later the entryphone buzzes.

COLE Ah, the old late-night buzz on the entryphone.

ELLEN She can see his face in the monitor. He's smoothing down his hair. She tells him she's going to bed. He's insistent. There's something he wants to talk about, it's important, he says it's about work –

COLE Work! Right.

ELLEN She believes him. She <u>wants</u> to believe him –

COLE – so she lets him in –

ELLEN – so she lets him in. He's distraught. What's the problem? She asks. I want to talk about us, he says.

COLE Aha.

ELLEN He tells her he's madly in love with her, has been since the day he first saw her, he thought he could deal with it, but things have changed.

COLE Changed how?

ELLEN Now he knows that she feels the same way about him –

COLE – oh excellent –

ELLEN – he's decided the time has come to 'admit to their feelings'. Only then can they 'move forward' –

COLE 'Move forward', excellent –

ELLEN She tells him he's mistaken. She respects him as a colleague, that's all. She has done nothing, nothing to suggest any more than that –

COLE – course she hasn't –

ELLEN – as she talks, he becomes increasingly distressed. The woman is starting to get frightened. Is he going to get violent? Will she have to call the police? To have her boss removed from her flat?

COLE Oooh messy –

ELLEN He doesn't become violent, but he becomes highly emotional. In the end he agrees to go but only after she promises to meet him in the morning. To discuss their 'future'.

COLE Oh. My. God.

ELLEN The woman is in shock. What's she to do? Make an official complaint? To her boss's boss? Who's worked with her boss for twenty years? Who's also a man?

Beat.

ELLEN She can't sleep, needless to say…in the early hours of the morning, she decides to give up her job –

COLE No way!

ELLEN She's writing her letter of resignation when the phone rings. It's her boss's boss, asking her to come in right away. Something's happened –

COLE Old Jack's gone ape, bollock naked in a meeting-room, howling at the moon! Yesssss!

Silence.

ELLEN This isn't about me and Jack.

COLE Course it isn't. Sorry, I forgot.

It's a <u>story</u>.

ELLEN Yes.

COLE So the woman doesn't resign.

ELLEN No.

COLE She gets promoted. Wahey. Happy ending.

ELLEN You think that's a happy ending?

COLE Course it is. That's why it's a good story...

COLE gets up.

...but I've got to tell you <u>Ellen</u>, no disrespect love, but I don't believe a fucking word of it. It's a fucking fantasy! She shagged the poor fucker, definitely, she shagged him and it wasn't even a mercy shag, it was a 'fuck him then fuck-him-up' shag. I'll fuck him, then I'll fuck his job, I'll fuck his salary –

ELLEN slaps COLE very hard.

I'll fuck his meetings –

ELLEN slaps him again, very hard.

I'll fuck his pension –

ELLEN slaps him again, very hard.

Yeah. Okay. Excellent.

Shaken, COLE sinks back on the sofa. ELLEN hands him a glass of water. COLE takes it, has a drink. ELLEN reaches out, touches COLE's cheek.

ELLEN Alright?

COLE nods. Drinks more water. Eventually:

COLE There's a bar near here. Treats.

ELLEN Yes?

COLE There's these dancers. We go there now and then. It's ironic. You know?

ELLEN I know.

COLE If the day pans out, we could go for a drink –

And **STRATTON** *hurries in.*

STRATTON Sorry, sorry. Lot of fuss about nothing as far as I can see, soon as IT are involved, everyone panics. So. Everything alright? Cole's been looking after you, I hope?

ELLEN Yes, he's been taking good care of me.

STRATTON Good, good. Have you had coffee?

ELLEN No, I'm fine thanks, but if you could tell me where the Ladies is –

STRATTON Of course, down the corridor and left, Lucy will show you.

ELLEN Thank you.

ELLEN exits.

STRATTON Everything alright, Cole?

COLE Yeah, yeah.

STRATTON You're very pink. Are you okay?

COLE Yeah, I'm good.

STRATTON And it was, it was alright with Ellen?

COLE Oh yeah.

STRATTON Did she – was she –

COLE – it's all good, Stratt. We bonded.

STRATTON Really? Seriously?

COLE Yeah, we're mates now.

STRATTON Good, good! You see? Basic social skills, Cole. They work.

COLE Yeah, they do, you're right.

STRATTON Did she talk about the contract?

COLE Yeah, she mentioned something.

STRATTON What?

COLE I dunno, something about Secondary Licensing.

STRATTON What? Secondary – ? Are you sure?

COLE Something like that, why?

> **STRATTON** *hurries to the desk, picks up his desk phone, punches in a number.*

What's the problem?

STRATTON *(into phone)* It's Stratton, is he there?

(…)

No, it's urgent, I've got to speak to him…

(…)

Yes, now!

(…)

Frank, listen – yes, we're –

(…)

No, we haven't actually started yet –

(…)

Because I had to leave the meeting to –

(…)

No, but she'll be back any minute. Look, while I was out of the room, she asked Cole about Secondary Licensing –

(…)

Yes. Exactly.

(…)

Well, get them down here –

(…)

Yes, soon as you can, Frank.

Hangs up.

COLE We're going for a drink later.

STRATTON What? Who?

COLE Me and Ellen. Thought I'd take her to Treats.

STRATTON Cole, I'm not in the mood for one of your jokes –

COLE No, she's bang up for it. You know what? There's more to that woman than meets the eye.

STRATTON Cole, remember what I said, don't –

And **ELLEN** *enters.* **COLE** *jumps to his feet.*

COLE *(to* **ELLEN***)* Alright?

ELLEN Fine, thank you. Sorry to keep you waiting.

COLE No problem, Ellen. You were saying, Stratt?

ELLEN *sits.*

STRATTON Nothing.

COLE Don't what, Stratt?

STRATTON Nothing, it's okay, nothing.

COLE Nothing. Alright.

This time **COLE** *sits down next to* **ELLEN**. **STRATTON** *hesitates, then sits down facing them.*

ELLEN I think we'd better press on, don't you?

STRATTON Absolutely.

COLE Absolutely.

ELLEN *and* **STRATTON** *refer to their laptops.* **COLE** *watches* **ELLEN**. *She notices.*

ELLEN Is everything alright, Cole?

COLE Absolutely, Ellen.

ELLEN Good.

STRATTON So, so where were we?

ELLEN Halfway down page forty-five –

STRATTON Page forty-five?

ELLEN Yes, relating to Third Party Costs.

STRATTON Third Party Costs?

COLE Jesus Stratt, are you deaf or something?

ELLEN Clause 2(c).

COLE *(speaking up)* Clause 2(c)!

STRATTON Yes, yes, here we are, got it. So what can I – what is the – the –

ELLEN I want to insert a phrase.

STRATTON You want to – okay, fine, good, what is the – what's the, the –

COLE Stop waffling, Stratt. She wants to insert a fucking phrase.

ELLEN I just want to insert the phrase 'and all other Third Party Costs' in line three, after 'deferred payments'.

STRATTON 'And all other Third Party Costs'. Right, let me just...

> **STRATTON** *reaches into an inside pocket, then remembers.*

Sorry, I need a, a –

> **STRATTON** *stands, is about to head for his desk.*

COLE Fuck's sake Stratt.

> **COLE** *is holding out a pen.* **STRATTON** *takes it. Looks at it.*

STRATTON *(looking at the pen)* Thank you.

> **STRATTON** *sits down again. Uncaps the pen. Starts to write.*

'And all other Third Party...'

> **STRATTON** *stops writing, looks at the pen.*

(to **COLE***)* Where did you get this?

COLE What?

STRATTON This pen. Where did you get it?

COLE Beth gave it to me.

> *Pause.*

STRATTON It's the same as mine.

COLE Oh really.

STRATTON *(To* **ELLEN***)* 'And all other Third Party Costs'?

ELLEN Yes.

> **STRATTON** *writes.*

After 'deferred payments'.

STRATTON *is looking at the pen again.*

STRATTON *(to* **COLE***)* Cole, can I, can I ask you – when exactly did Beth give this to you?

COLE I dunno. The other night.

STRATTON *(to* **ELLEN***)* Sorry. After 'deferred payments'?

ELLEN Yes.

> **STRATTON** *makes a note.*

STRATTON *(to* **COLE***)* The other night?

ELLEN I'm sorry, are we discussing the contract, or –

STRATTON Ellen, excuse me, one minute.

To **COLE**.

Cole?

COLE Yeah, the other night in Treats. What's the problem, Stratt? Aren't I allowed a pen like yours? Is it like a hierarchy thing? The hierarchy of writing instruments?

STRATTON No, no, it's – it's –

COLE *(to* **ELLEN***)* I split with my girlfriend.

ELLEN I'm sorry to hear that.

COLE Don't be, I'm delighted. Anyway, she gave me the pen before it all kicked off. So what you do you think? Should I give it back? What would you say is the etiquette on that, Ellen?

ELLEN I would say it was a matter for your conscience.

COLE Umm. I like that. Got a nice retro feel to it. 'A matter for my conscience' –

ELLEN So. Moving on, if we may –

COLE – but you know what?

STRATTON Cole –

COLE – I think I'm going to keep it.

STRATTON Cole?

COLE Yes, Stratton?

Pause.

What?

STRATTON I – I –

Pause. Then **FRANK** *enters carrying a document.*

FRANK *Bonjour tout le monde, salut,* forgive me for interrupting the flow, but I come with urgent news from the tenth floor, news both good and bad. Ellen, are these hooligans looking after you?

ELLEN Yes, they are, thank you.

STRATTON What news, Frank?

FRANK Well, the air may be rarified up there, the tone a mite sombre, 'uneasy lies the head' and so on, but they love what you're doing down here and could not be more excited. That is the good news.

STRATTON And the bad?

FRANK holds up the document in his hand.

FRANK Some amendments relating to Secondary Licensing...

FRANK hands the document to **STRATTON**.

...which I bring to you with grovelling apologies from the tenth floor. I am assured that they are minimal, merely a question of 'phrasing'.

ELLEN A question of phrasing?

FRANK Yes, with grovelling apologies.

> **STRATTON** *holds out the document for* **ELLEN**.

Ellen, I suggest you use one of our conference rooms to go over the amendments in private.

> *Pause.* **ELLEN** *takes the document from* **STRATTON**.

Unless of course you want to take them over the road and confer.

ELLEN That won't be necessary.

> **COLE** *stands.*

COLE I'll show you the –

FRANK No, Cole. Stratton, will you take Ms David to the conference room on the sixth floor please –

COLE It's alright, I'll take her –

FRANK No, Cole. You stay here. Stratton.

Please.

> **STRATTON** *stands.*

STRATTON Right. Of course.

> **ELLEN** *stands, follows* **STRATTON** *to the door.* **STRATTON** *opens the door.* **ELLEN** *pauses, holds up the document.*

ELLEN This is… I know what's going on here. I'm not impressed.

FRANK What can I say? I am merely the –

ELLEN Don't. Don't blame it on the 'tenth floor'. It makes you look weak.

> **ELLEN** *exits followed by* **STRATTON**.

COLE Ooooh Frank, she's got you down.

FRANK Talk to me, Cole.

Beat.

COLE Okay, so I had this teacher, Miss Farley. Everybody hated her. She wore black. Cardigans, skirts. She was probably what? Forty? But to me, then, she was ancient. She'd come and stand by my desk, point at my work. Big white hands with blue veins. I could smell her, Polo mints and fags, disgusting.

Beat.

And I'd get a major hard-on. <u>Major</u>.

Beat.

Very confusing for a young lad trembling on the brink of sexual awareness, wouldn't you say Frank?

Beat.

I never told anyone. I couldn't. Getting a boner off Miss Farley, that would've been <u>so</u> gay.

Silence.

FRANK Talk to me, Cole.

COLE 'Trembling on the brink of sexual awareness' – I'm starting to sound like you, Frank. What an influence you've been on me. Like a father. Almost.

FRANK Talk to me about the break-in on the fourth floor.

COLE What?

FRANK Talk to me about breaking into Beth's desk. Talk to me about hacking in to her computer.

COLE Fuck off.

FRANK They're going through the CCTV footage now.

COLE First off, I didn't do it. Second off, the cameras haven't been recording since the cut-backs, everybody knows that. So fuck you in a fucking hat, Frank.

FRANK One in four, Cole. One in four cameras are recording. Maybe you were lucky. Maybe you were out of shot.

Beat.

Either way, we have to address this now. We have to make a pre-emptive strike. I can talk to them on the tenth floor, tell them there are mitigating circumstances. I'll tell them you were under extreme emotional pressure. I'll tell them you have 'issues'.

Beat.

I might be able to make this go away.

COLE Why would you do that?

FRANK Because I want to keep you on my team.

COLE Because you love me, right?

FRANK Yes, I love my team. I love you all.

Silence.

COLE I saw them, Frank.

FRANK You saw what?

COLE The emails. On Beth's computer. I saw the emails.

Beat.

Frank. Really. You old saucepot. What were you thinking?

FRANK Those emails are relating to work and work alone.

COLE You? Emailing Beth about work? Purrlease!

FRANK There is nothing in those emails that could be construed as inappropriate.

COLE Well, it's all a question of 'perception', isn't it?

FRANK You'll find it's my perception that counts on the tenth floor.

COLE Not sure about that, Frankie boy.

FRANK Oh, they hate you up there.

COLE No, they're frightened, that's all. The world's changing too fast for them. And you, Frank. Whooosh! End of. All gone. Cue music.

Beat.

It's alright, I know you're not doing her, Frank. Someone is, I still don't know who, but it isn't you. She doesn't like you Frank, she thinks you're a perv. I told her, no, he isn't a perv, he's just old, but they're one and the same thing to her you see, there's no talking her out of it.

FRANK And you really believe her, don't you? What a sweet, trusting boy you are, Cole, under all that foul – mouthed urchin swagger. Just a sweet, anxious boy hiding his darling erection under the desk, hoping teacher will come along and finish him off –

And **COLE** *punches* **FRANK** *in the stomach.* **FRANK** *collapses on a sofa, doubled up, winded.*

STRATTON *enters.*

STRATTON Sandwiches or sushi, what do you think? Shall I get Lucy to order something now? Or is it too early? What does everyone want? What about you, Frank? Or are you having lunch on the tenth floor?

STRATTON goes to his desk, sits, checks his watch. Then notices FRANK's discomfort.

Frank, are you alright?

FRANK *sits up straight with an effort.*

FRANK Stomach cramps.

STRATTON Stomach cramps?

FRANK I'm alright.

STRATTON Did you – did you eat something –

FRANK I'm alright, Stratton –

STRATTON I could send Lucy out for something, because you don't look –

COLE Stop fussing, Stratt, for fuck's sake.

STRATTON What's going on? Has something happened?

FRANK Everything is absolutely... Cole, what's that phrase that gives me cancer?

COLE 'Hunky-dory'.

FRANK Exactly.

STRATTON Well, it doesn't feel like it. Cole?

No response.

FRANK Cole and I had a slight disagreement. Which we have resolved. Haven't we Cole?

STRATTON A disagreement?

COLE It's personal, Stratt, alright?

STRATTON Personal? <u>Personal</u>?

FRANK And is no longer a problem. It's gone away. Hasn't it, Cole?

COLE I'm not sure, Frank. I'm not sure it has gone away.

STRATTON Look, sorry, but this is –

FRANK – none of your business, Stratton.

STRATTON I – I – I –

COLE Shut the fuck up, Stratt.

FRANK Do you know what you've got here, Cole? You've got one of those moments.

Beat.

One of those moments in which you have to make a choice. Which is it to be, old sock? The High Road or the Low Road? The Sunny Side of the Street or the Vale of Tears? Scary stuff, Cole. Grown-up stuff. Are you up to it? Are you – I think I can ask the question here, among friends – are you <u>man</u> enough?

ELLEN enters, holding the document.

Ah, Ellen. We were just discussing the decision-making process.

ELLEN Really.

FRANK Some say that decisions are best made instantaneously. 'First thought, best thought' and so on. They say that 'mulling things over' and 'thinking things through' leads only to chaos and confusion. What's your view?

ELLEN I don't know, I'll have to mull it over.

STRATTON I was, I was going to order in some lunch. Sandwiches, or sushi perhaps, there's a very good place –

ELLEN Not for me, thanks.

ELLEN sits, tosses the document down on the table. Crosses her legs.

I am very disappointed – no, let me rephrase that. I am actually very <u>angry</u> –

FRANK Ellen, if I could just –

ELLEN Do you mind? May I finish what I was saying?

Silence.

Thank you. This…

ELLEN *picks up the document, tosses it down again.*

…this is – I mean, are you <u>serious</u>? Really? You want <u>all</u> the Secondary Licensing? <u>All</u> of it?

STRATTON I – I – I –

ELLEN Am I supposed to flutter my eyelashes like a good girl and sign away the whole package, just like that – ?

STRATTON No, the thing is –

ELLEN – and you know what the really insulting thing is? –

STRATTON – can I just – may I –

ELLEN – you would not have done this to Jack Holland.

COLE Actually –

FRANK Shut up, Cole.

ELLEN Good old Jack. Your 'mate'.

Beat.

This…

The document.

…is about putting me in my place, this is macho point-scoring, nothing more.

COLE Dick-swinging, Frank, is what she's saying.

FRANK Ellen, I can only apologise on behalf of the tenth floor. They are past their prime, testosterone levels are declining, and yes, they are prone to outbursts of inappropriate machismo –

COLE Dick-swinging by the dickless, Frankie –

STRATTON I – we – we could perhaps – I would be happy to –

And the phone on **STRATTON**'s *desk rings. Nobody moves for a beat. Then* **STRATTON** *goes over to his desk and answers it.*

(into phone) Lucy, we're in the middle of –

(…)

What?

(…)

What, <u>now</u>? Are you sure?

(…)

But did they say what –

(…)

Well, it's very, I mean, we're in the middle of –

(…)

I see.

(…)

Alright. Thank you, Lucy.

STRATTON *hangs up, then:*

Frank, they want to see you on the tenth floor.

FRANK I'll go up shortly –

STRATTON No, they want to see you now.

FRANK Well, will you ask Lucy to tell them, ever so politely, that I am in the middle of a meeting and will be up as soon as it's over.

STRATTON They want you now. This minute. You too, Cole.

COLE Me?

STRATTON Both of you. Right away.

Beat.

Frank, what's going on?

FRANK *Calme-toi*, Stratton. Ellen, so sorry but it seems Cole and I must attend another meeting, and it would help us, that's to say Cole and me, if you could give us some idea of your intentions.

ELLEN My intentions?

FRANK Yes. Is there the slenderest chance, do you think, that we could find a way to heal the damage done by this unwonted interference –

The document.

– and retrace our steps?

ELLEN You're leaving this meeting to go to another meeting?

FRANK Yes. And I sincerely apologise.

ELLEN A meeting that is obviously more important than this one? And you want to know my 'intentions'?

FRANK It would be most helpful, yes.

ELLEN Well, I'm still in this meeting, and I have to say that I resent your crude attempt to pressurise me, so no, Frank, I will not give you any indication of my 'intentions'.

FRANK Of course. And once again I apologise. Cole?

COLE *doesn't move.*

Cole, come along.

COLE *doesn't move.*

STRATTON Frank –

FRANK Later, Stratton.

> *To* **COLE**.

> I need your help, Cole.

> **COLE** *doesn't move.*

> And you need mine. Let's go and sort this out. As a team, yes?

> **COLE** *eventually stands. Goes to the door which* **FRANK** *holds open for him.*

> *(to* **COLE***)* Alright?

COLE Hunky-dory, Frank.

FRANK Dear boy, you are such a tease.

> **FRANK** *and* **COLE** *exit.* **ELLEN** *and* **STRATTON** *sitting opposite each other on the sofas.*

STRATTON I'm sorry, I – I…

ELLEN Have you any idea what's going on here?

STRATTON With them? No. No, I don't.

> *Beat.*

> But what Frank was saying…

ELLEN Yes?

STRATTON About negotiating some sort of compromise –

ELLEN Negotiating?

> **ELLEN** *leans forward, picks up the document, holds it aloft.*

> Negotiating on the basis of this piece of, of – blatant robbery? Absolutely not.

ELLEN *tosses the document on the table, opens a bottle of mineral water, pours for herself and* **STRATTON**. *Drinks, sits back. Crosses her legs.*

Over the road they've already lost confidence okay? You know, and I know, that once upon a time there was a good deal here. But in their eyes, it's been seriously compromised by Jack Holland's behaviour. It's a question of perception.

STRATTON Perception, yes.

ELLEN So what I cannot do is go back over the road and tell them I have signed off on the deal having made concessions. Any concessions whatsoever, Stratton.

STRATTON Yes. Yes, of course, I – I –

ELLEN So we're done here. I'm not going to negotiate anything, I'm not going to sign anything, okay? For business reasons primarily, but also on principle.

STRATTON On principle?

ELLEN Stratton, I think you're a good person, a 'good bloke'.

STRATTON Well, I – I –

ELLEN – but you've been seriously let down by senior management – yes, we've all been there, – but <u>you</u>, you have also been let down by your colleagues.

STRATTON My colleagues?

ELLEN Yes, I'm talking about the spirit in which these negotiations have been conducted.

Beat.

Do you understand? I'm talking about the way in which I've been treated. That's to say ill – mannered, obtuse and, on at least one occasion, abusive in the extreme –

Then the phone on **STRATTON** *'s desk rings.* **STRATTON** *lets it ring for a beat or two.*

STRATTON I'm sorry.

ELLEN *gestures: be my guest.* **STRATTON** *gets up, answers the call.*

(into phone) Lucy, I'm still –

(...)

What?

(...)

But – but –

(...)

Alright, I'll, I'll talk to her.

(to **ELLEN** *)* Sorry, will you give me a minute.

(...)

(into phone) Hallo? Are you –

(...)

No, I'm still in this meeting –

(...)

No, I told you darling, I had to turn it off because of the meeting –

(...)

No, not because –

ELLEN *puts away her laptop, quietly prepares to leave during the following:*

(into phone) Please, Vanessa, not that again, please –

(...)

Where are you? It sounds like –

(...)

Is that Claudia? Why isn't she at school?

(...)

Why did you do that? We talked about –

(...)

Just let me talk to her.

(...)

Hallo, sweetheart. What are you –

(...)

I know, Mummy's upset because –

(...)

Don't worry, sweetheart. I'm in a meeting now, but as soon as it's over, I'll come and get you –

(...)

No, she's just in one of her funny –

(...)

Straight away, but first sweetheart, you've got to tell me where you are –

ELLEN, *about to leave the office, pauses. Looks back at* **STRATTON**.

(into phone) What's the hotel called?

(...)

Claudia, is that the TV? Could you turn it down, I can't –

(...)

I need to know where the hotel is, so I can –

(...)

Sweetheart, tell her I want to talk to her –

(…)

No sweetheart, I really didn't do that, Mummy's just in one of her funny –

(…)

Claudia, don't –

(…)

Don't! Let me, let me…

Pause. **STRATTON** *hangs up. He leans over his desk, supporting himself with his arms, head bowed. Hyperventilating.*

ELLEN *puts down her bag, goes over to* **STRATTON**.

ELLEN Are you alright?

No response.

Stratton?

STRATTON I'm okay.

ELLEN Maybe you'd better sit down.

STRATTON Yes, I think I'll sit down.

ELLEN *leads* **STRATTON** *over to the sofa. He sits.* **ELLEN** *hands him a glass of water. He drinks.*

ELLEN Alright?

STRATTON Would you mind staying for a minute or two?

ELLEN Alright.

ELLEN *sits.* **STRATTON**'s *breathing starts to ease. He laughs.*

What?

STRATTON I was just remembering…

ELLEN Yes?

STRATTON Fourteen years ago I was going out with this girl, we'd been going out for a year, we got on well some of the time, but she was often very upset, very angry with me, and I could never work out why…

Beat.

…but she was very attached to me, despite the fact that I upset her. <u>Very</u> attached to me…it seemed that the more I upset her, the more attached she became. So I was very, very unhappy. And I decided that I'd have to split up with her. Which of course I dreaded because I knew it would make her…very upset.

STRATTON *drinks some more water.*

But I was determined to do it, so one evening I went to her flat to tell her.

Beat.

It was as if she knew what I was going to say because she was already – she was already very upset. We'd been out with friends the night before and I'd said something, or done something, which had upset her. She said 'How could you humiliate me like that, in front of everyone?'. The fact that I couldn't remember saying or doing whatever it was upset her even more. I apologised. She shouted at me 'I don't want an apology, I want an explanation!'

Beat.

I'd brought a bottle of wine with me because I knew I'd need a drink. She insisted on opening it.

Her back was to me, she was crying, her whole body was shaking while she tried to open the bottle…then she let out a terrible – a terrible cry, and turned round and I saw that the corkscrew was impaled in the ball of her thumb and she was trying, she was trying to pull it out...

Beat.

...so I rushed to help her...

Beat.

...and then I realised that she wasn't trying to pull the corkscrew out, she was digging it in even deeper...

Silence.

...so I grabbed her, I grabbed her hand and tried to stop her digging it in, and finally she let go and I managed to get the corkscrew out. There was blood. She was crying and crying, so...

Silence.

...so I asked her to marry me.

Silence.

To stop her crying. And she did. And she held on to me very tight, and there was this, this explosion in my head...and it dawned on me, yes, I must love her. I must. It's the – it's the only explanation for all this pain.

ELLEN I'm sorry –

STRATTON No, no, no, it's alright, you don't have to...it's alright.

STRATTON *drinks some more water.*

Ellen.

ELLEN Yes?

STRATTON I want to ask you something.

ELLEN Yes?

STRATTON Would you have signed off on the original deal? Without the amendments?

ELLEN Yes, I would. That's what I came here to do.

Beat.

But that isn't going to happen, is it?

Beat.

STRATTON I've got the original contracts over there, on my desk. We could do it. You and I, we could do it.

ELLEN Are you serious?

STRATTON Oh yes.

ELLEN What would the tenth floor say? What would Frank say?

STRATTON *stands up, goes to his desk, picks up two contracts.*

STRATTON It's a good idea, isn't it?

ELLEN It's a fantastic idea.

STRATTON And it's a great deal.

ELLEN Yes, it's a great deal but –

STRATTON Never mind Frank. Never mind the tenth floor. Never mind over the road. Fuck 'em.

STRATTON *sits down next to* **ELLEN** *with the contracts.*

ELLEN Can I ask you something?

STRATTON Anything.

ELLEN It's none of my business, but you seem to be under some sort of personal pressure. In your life?

Beat.

I mean, are you sure you should be making a decision like this now? Bearing in the mind the possible consequences?

STRATTON Do you care?

ELLEN Yes, I do.

> *A moment.* **STRATTON** *and* **ELLEN** *looking each other in the eye.*

STRATTON Thank you. Really. But I know what I'm doing.

> *Beat.*

Frank will be back any minute.

ELLEN Then let's do it.

> **STRATTON** *opens one of the contracts at the relevant pages.*

STRATTON The top copy is yours.

> **STRATTON** *pats his pockets – no pen.*

> **ELLEN** *takes a pen from her bag, holds it up.*

STRATTON *(indicating)* You sign here. And here. And then here. Now my copy.

> **STRATTON** *opens another contract, opens it, hands it to* **ELLEN**.

Here and here. And here.

> **ELLEN** *signs.*

ELLEN The tenth floor, over the road – they don't deserve us, that's the truth of the matter. Your turn.

> **ELLEN** *hands* **STRATTON** *the pen and the contracts.* **STRATTON** *is about to sign. He pauses. His breathing is becoming heavier again.*

Are you alright?

STRATTON *doesn't answer.*

Stratton?

No answer.

Are you...

ELLEN *glances anxiously back at the door.*

...are you going to sign?

STRATTON Would you, would you come out with me for coffee?

ELLEN What?

STRATTON It's such a lovely day. We could sit outside, in the sun, and talk.

ELLEN That would be nice. After you've signed the contract?

STRATTON I think it's important that we talk <u>before</u> I sign the contract.

Pause.

ELLEN Are you saying –

STRATTON I need to talk to you –

ELLEN – are you saying that you won't sign unless I come out with you? For 'coffee'?

STRATTON We need to talk. Before I sign the contract.

ELLEN 'We need to talk'? Wait a minute, are you, is this –

STRATTON To talk, that's all. Please.

ELLEN Is this a <u>proposition?</u>

STRATTON Please.

A moment while **ELLEN** *regards* **STRATTON**. *Then she stands.*

ELLEN Forget it. Can I just say for the record, that I'm –

STRATTON Sorry, I – sorry, I wasn't, I was just –

ELLEN Can I just say how –

STRATTON It was, I was, it was a sincere –

ELLEN Really, <u>really</u> –

STRATTON Sorry, sorry. I'm signing, okay? Here and here and here. Okay? Now my copy. Here and here... and here.

STRATTON *finishes signing, stands, hands a contract to* **ELLEN**.

I'm sorry.

ELLEN Of course you are.

STRATTON No, really. I am.

There's something unfamiliar in **STRATTON**'*s voice. A hardness, perhaps.* **ELLEN** *looks at him for a moment.*

ELLEN If you're expecting me to throw myself at your feet in gratitude, forget it.

ELLEN *gathers up her stuff* –

Goodbye, Stratton.

– and exits.

STRATTON *stands motionless. The deskphone rings.* **STRATTON** *goes over to the desk, looks at the phone for a moment, then picks it, whacks it against the desk. It keeps on ringing.* **STRATTON** *chucks it on the floor and stamps on it. It continues ringing.* **STRATTON** *stamps on it until it stops. It's amazingly resilient.*

Then **STRATTON** *picks up his computer, throws that across the office.*

STRATTON *rips his jacket off, throws it after the computer. Claws at his shirt and tie, popping the buttons, shredding the cloth –*

– then sees the can of air freshener, still on the desk. **STRATTON** *picks it up, sprays it in his eyes. Cries out.*

STRATTON, *in a blind frenzy, careers about the office, bouncing off the walls.*

FRANK *enters, followed by* **COLE**. *They circle* **STRATTON** *warily, waiting for a chance to grab him. Which they finally do.* **STRATTON** *resists them at first. Then gradually calms down. Clasped in* **FRANK** *and* **COLE**'s *arms.*

FRANK It's alright now.

There, there.

It's alright now.

There's a good little soldier.

Blackout.

FOUR

Evening. A gloomy passage at the rear of TREATS, a lap– dancing club.

Left, a door to the street with an illuminated 'EXIT' sign. A sign saying 'TOILETS'.

Right, a door into the club. Thumping music audible from the other side.

Plastic beer crates are stacked along the wall. **STRATTON** *is sitting on one of them, an empty champagne glass in one hand, handkerchief in the other.* **STRATTON** *dabs at his eyes with the handkerchief.*

The music is suddenly louder for a moment as the door to the club opens and **COLE** *enters, beer in hand.*

COLE Stratt?

> **COLE** *sits next to* **STRATTON***, puts his arm round him.*

Stratt, I don't know what to say!

> **COLE** *clinks his bottle against* **STRATTON***'s empty glass, drinks.*

You alright then?

STRATTON Yes, yes, I'm –

COLE Cos you are top fucking geeze mate. Seriously. And I just want to say, anything I said earlier, it was just, you know, wossername, okay?

STRATTON Well, thanks, I – I...

COLE *gives* STRATTON *a hug.*

COLE Love you to bits, man. Truth.

COLE *stands.*

Are you coming through? Frank's even running a tab! Can you believe it?

STRATTON What, what happened with Beth?

COLE Beth? Beth's gone.

STRATTON Gone?

COLE Gone. As in 'gone'. Escorted from the premises. Didn't you hear? She was bang at it, according to Frank.

STRATTON Bang at it?

COLE You know. Shagging in the offices, nicking stuff. Ask Frank. Anyway, he's sorted it, thank fuck. What a piece of work she turned out to be!

Pause.

Are you coming or what? We've got the little Ukrainian, and the blonde with the piercings, we've got them for an hour on Frank's tab.

STRATTON Later maybe.

COLE *heads for the door to the club, pauses, raises his beer.*

COLE Hey. Stratt the Man!

A loud blast of music as COLE *goes into the club. A beat, then* STRATTON *fumbles in an inside pocket as his phone rings.*

STRATTON *(into phone)* Hallo –

(…)

No –

(...)

No, not yet...

(...)

No, I'm in a meeting.

(...)

It's a different meeting.

(...)

As soon as it's over, Vanessa.

(...)

Yes, as soon as it's over.

(...)

Is she in bed?

(...)

Vanessa, is she in bed?

(...)

Alright. So tell her goodnight from Daddy. Tell her Daddy will take her to school tomorrow.

(...)

I've got the day off.

(...)

Well, I have.

(...)

Yes, it is nice.

(...)

Does there have to be a reason?

A loud blast of music as **FRANK** *comes in from the club.*
A bottle of champagne in one hand, glass in the other.

(into phone) I just decided to take the day off, that's all –

(…)

Music? What music?

(…)

Well, it's not coming from this end.

(…)

I can't talk anymore –

(…)

I'm hanging up now, Vanessa.

Hangs up.

FRANK *fills up* **STRATTON** *'s glass, tops up his own.*

FRANK So. I take it the wanderer has returned.

STRATTON Yes.

FRANK Is this a frequent occurrence? The phone call from the airport hotel? The threat of flight?

STRATTON It's happened before, yes.

FRANK Stratton, why don't you talk to me about these things? I'm mystified, and not a little hurt. Because I do love you, you know, in my twisted way. You could talk to me to your heart's content. You could talk to me 'till the cows come home, long after they come home, if you so desired.

Pause.

Though I doubt I could say anything instructive, I doubt I could give you 'good advice'. But that's not really the point, is it? My darling wife used to say 'Frank, you have many faults, but you are a good listener'. She would talk and I would listen. Well, that's not strictly true. I wasn't always listening. Hardly ever, in fact. But I gave every appearance of listening, and that's what matters. She talked, and I appeared to listen, and it was a source of great comfort to her in her darkest hours. Of which there were many towards the end.

Pause.

I'm going to take you to Huntley and Wakes, get Mr Price to cut you a suit. A wool-cashmere mix, say. Something with a whiff of decadence. My treat.

STRATTON You don't have to do that, Frank.

FRANK No, but I'm minded to make a 'gesture', so indulge me.

Drinks.

Everything disappoints in the end, Stratton, particularly if you're of a romantic disposition. Money, love, sex. Sex! Don't start me! It's a shitstorm out there, Stratton, a raging shitstorm of disappointment, and one might as well face it in a decent suit.

FRANK *heads for the door to the club, pauses.*

Are you going to join the party?

STRATTON In a minute.

FRANK *raises his glass.*

FRANK Here's to you, old sock.

A blast of music as **FRANK** *exits into the club.* **STRATTON** *drinks, tops up his glass from the bottle that* **FRANK** *has left.*

The 'exit' door opens. **ELLEN** *stands on the threshold.* **STRATTON** *looks up, sees her. He eventually gets to his feet.*

ELLEN *enters.*

ELLEN The circle-jerk in full swing, is it?

STRATTON Would you like a drink? I'll get you a…

ELLEN *takes the bottle, drinks from it.*

STRATTON …glass.

ELLEN So. What larks, eh?

Beat.

There I was, all hot and bothered about last minute amendments. 'This is outrageous, I'm not giving away all this!' And guess what, that's exactly what I end up doing!

Beat.

So. Plenty of revenue for everyone over the first two years. But then, one by one, the secondary rights revert to you, creeping away on their tippy-toes, ever so quietly, and our revenue dwindles, penny by penny, pound by pound, until…it dries up altogether! Fabulous. Well done, you!

Beat.

The first commandment: 'Always be closest to the till'.

Beat.

And the joke is, I was going to query the Secondary Licensing, I really was.

ELLEN *takes another swig from the bottle.*

But then there was that business with the pen. My oh my, the famous pen! 'Where did you get this pen? It looks like my pen!' Fabulous.

STRATTON Actually, that was –

ELLEN And then the phone call?

'Sweetheart, where are you? Tell Daddy where you are, sweetheart!' Was it Frank on the other end? Hilarious –

STRATTON Actually, no, that was –

ELLEN Oh, no disclaimers, please. No false modesty.

Beat. **STRATTON** *sits back down.*

STRATTON I tried to warn you.

ELLEN What, 'Come out for coffee'? That was a <u>warning</u>, was it?

Beat.

'Oh, what a lovely day, let's go and sit in the sun, I really want to 'talk".

Beat.

That was a <u>warning</u>?

STRATTON Yes.

ELLEN Well, silly me, how could I possibly have misread <u>that</u>?

STRATTON I suppose it's a question of perception.

ELLEN Oh fuck off, Stratton.

STRATTON Yes, well, I – I –

ELLEN Just fuck right fucking off.

Silence.

I came here tonight to ask you if there wasn't some way in which…

STRATTON What?

ELLEN Some way in which we could…restructure the schedule, maybe adjust the cut-off dates. Something your people on the tenth floor wouldn't object to.

Beat.

Something I can take back over the road. Something to soften the blow. Anything.

Beat.

Because otherwise I'm finished.

ELLEN *takes another swig of champagne.*

That's why I came here.

Beat.

To ask if there's anything you can do –

STRATTON Did you fuck Jack Holland?

ELLEN What?

STRATTON Did you fuck Jack Holland?

ELLEN I beg your pardon?

STRATTON Did you?

Silence.

ELLEN No.

Silence.

Yes.

Silence.

No.

Silence.

What's the right answer, Stratton?

STRATTON Did you?

ELLEN Does it really matter?

STRATTON *doesn't answer.*

No, I did not fuck Jack Holland. Now will you help me?

Silence.

STRATTON Dance for me.

ELLEN What?

STRATTON Dance for me.

They regard each other, not moving.

Fade to black.

End

Property List

Computer (p1)
Phones (p1)
Laptop bag (p1)
Mobile (p1)
Can of air freshener (p1)
Earphones (p3)
Shoulder bag (p3)
Laptop (p3)
Mobile (p3)
Pen (p15)
Mobile (p19)
Air freshener (p19)
Magazines (p21)
Glasses, water (p21)
Laptop (p21)
Laptop bag (p24)
Laminated visitors bag (p24)
Laptop (p25)
Air freshener (p45)
Laptops (p49)
Bottle of mineral water (p52)
Glass of water (p58)
Pen (p62)
Document (p64)
Watch (p69)
Bottle of mineral water (p75)
Glass of water (p79)
Two contracts (p82)
Pen (p83)
Plastic beer crates (p87)
Empty champagne class (p87)
Handkerchief (p87)
Beer (p87)
Bottle of champagne (p89)

Glass (p89)

Costume
Stratton – suit, tie (p1)
Cole – casually dressed (p3)
Frank – impeccably suited and booted (p10)
Cole – coat (p23)
Ellen – soberly dressed (p24)

Lighting

Blackout (p18)
Blackout (p42)
Blackout (p86)
Evening. A gloomy passage at the rear of TREATS, a lap dancing club (p87)
Illuminated EXIT sign (p87)
A sign saying TOILETS (p87)
Fade to black (p95)

Sound/Effects

Desk phone rings (p3)
Stratton's mobile rings (p13)
Stratton's desk phone rings (p15)
Phone on Stratton's desk rings (p23)
Stratton's mobile rings (p32)
Phone on Stratton's desk rings (p48)
Phone on Stratton's desk rings (p50)
Phone on Stratton's desk rings (p72)
Phone on Stratton's desk rings. Stratton lets it ring for a beat or two (p76)
Desk phone rings...it keeps on ringing...it continues ringing...Stratton stamps on it until it stops (p85)
Thumping music audible (p87)

The music is suddenly louder for a moment as the door to
the club opens (p87)
Loud blast of music (p88)
Phone rings (p88)
A loud blast of music (p89)
Blast of music (p91)

Lightning Source UK Ltd.
Milton Keynes UK
UKOW06f1831020216

267628UK00004B/13/P